P9-CJK-970

Sunset

ideas for great

PATIOS AND DECKS

By Scott Atkinson
and the Editors of Sunset Books

Sunset Books ■ Menlo Park, California

Sunset Books

vice president, general manager:
Richard A. Smeby

vice president, editorial director:
Bob Doyle

production director:
Lory Day

art director:
Vasken Guiragossian

Staff for this book:

developmental editor:
Linda J. Selden

copy editor:
Marcia Williamson

design:
Barbara Vick

page layout:
Kathy Avanzino Barone

illustrations:
Bill Oetinger
Mark Pechenik

principal photographer:
Philip Harvey

photo director:
JoAnn Masaoka Van Atta

production coordinator:
Patricia S. Williams
10 9 8 7 6 5

First printing January 2000
*Copyright © 2000, 1994, Sunset Publishing Corporation,
Menlo Park, CA 94025. Second edition. All rights
reserved, including the right of reproduction in whole or
in part in any form.*

ISBN 0-376-01409-1
Library of Congress Catalog Card Number: 99-60452
Printed in the United States.

*For additional copies of Ideas for Great Patios & Decks
or any other Sunset Book, call 1-800-526-5111.
Or see our web site at: www.sunsetbooks.com*

*Cover: Twin arched arbors frame the way to a front-yard patio.
Landscape architect: The Berger Partnership. Cover design by
Vasken Guiragossian. Photography by Philip Harvey. Photo
direction by JoAnn Masaoka Van Atta.*

An outdoor adventure

This newly-revised title in Sunset's popular "Ideas for Great..." series is crammed full of ideas and information to help you dream, then design the patio or deck of your choice.

Vibrant photos show the latest in landscapes, from tiny garden retreats of rustic brick to sweeping, multilevel decks in redwood and mahogany. Clear examples allow you to window-shop through the latest offerings in flagstone, lumber, and man-made decking materials. When you're ready to dig in, you can also take advantage of our solid introduction to patio planning and design.

Many landscaping professionals, manufacturers, and homeowners shared ideas with us or allowed us to photograph their spaces. We'd especially like to thank ASN Natural Stone of San Francisco and Eco Timber of Berkeley, California. Chugrad McAndrews spent many hours ably assisting with location photography.

Design credits for specific photos are listed on pages 110–111.

contents

deck, patio, or both?

IN THE QUEST for more living space, there's one spot we often overlook: outside. What better way to take the heat off interior traffic, bring the outdoors in, and frame dramatic views than to build or expand an outdoor hardscape?

Your outdoor room might be classic and formal or fluid and naturalistic. You may be yearning for an inviting entertainment space, a remote private refuge, a restorative spa, or simply for a flat spot for sunbathing and stargazing. Or maybe you want it all. You needn't settle for that boring patio slab. Interior design ideas are migrating outdoors and new shapes, colors, textures, and amenities abound.

First things first: would you prefer a patio or a deck? Sometimes it's simply a matter of site or style. Deck lumber is durable and resilient underfoot, and it won't store heat the way other materials can. Decks can tame sloping, bumpy, or poorly draining ground. Designs and materials are dancing new steps. Hardwoods add a furniture-like elegance; man-made and recycled products are also on the rise.

Patios, on the other hand, lend an unmatched sense of permanence and tradition to a formal garden or house design. You might choose unit masonry such as traditional brick, ceramic tile, or elegant stone. Concrete pavers are rising stars, and they're easy for the do-it-yourselfer to install. And don't rule out concrete; you'll discover there are lots of jazzy techniques for coloring, texturing, and softening the familiar slab. Loose materials are yet another option.

Or why not combine both patio and deck in one multifaceted design? A blend of masonry and wood allows great flexibility in space, texture, and finished height.

On the following pages you'll find solutions for large lots, tiny lots, and hilly lots. The first chapter, "A Planning Primer," will walk you through the evaluation of your present site and help you refine your thoughts. For a tour of patio styles and solutions, take a good look at the photos in the next chapter, "Great Patios and Decks." For shopping tips and pointers, see the third chapter, "A Shopper's Guide."

And since summer's always just around the corner, isn't now the time to get started?

A PLANNING PRIMER

As fun as it is to daydream about the new outdoor living space you are going to create, careful planning is what will make the dream become reality. **To choose the best site,** you'll first need to study your property's orientation, its topography, and its weather patterns and produce a base map. That's where this chapter begins. **Comparing various options** in design and materials will help you visualize what you want; browse through the photos in Chapter Two, "Great Patios and Decks," for ideas. For help evaluating materials, see pages 91–109. **Return to this chapter** for both solid design guidelines and a guided walk through the planning process. When you've finished, you should have working drawings in hand. Use these to communicate with professionals or, if you're so inclined, to build the project yourself.

taking stock

THE PATH *to a comfortable new patio or deck begins right outside your door. In the following pages we take a look at basic site strategies and consider some important weather factors. Then we show you how to make a detailed base map of your property.*

What are your options?

Many people regard a patio or deck as a simple rectangle off the back door. But why not consider a succession of patios and level changes connected by steps, or a secluded "getaway" deck to make use of an attractive corner of your property? Perhaps you could even reclaim a forsaken side yard. Some of the possibilities are discussed below.

L- AND U-SHAPED SPACES. A house with an L or U shape almost cries out for a patio or deck. Surrounding house walls already form an enclosure; a privacy screen and a decorative structure overhead (such as an arbor, pergola, or even a simple roof) complete the "outdoor room." Often such a site can be gracefully accessed from several different parts of the house.

WRAPAROUNDS. A flat lot is a natural candidate for a wraparound patio, which enlarges the apparent size of the house while allowing access from any room along its course. If there's a gentle grade, rise above it with a slightly elevated wraparound deck, which the Japanese call an engawa.

DETACHED SITES. Perfect for serving as a quiet retreat, a detached patio or deck can be built on either a flat or a sloping lot and looks very much at home in a casual cottage-garden landscape. Create access to it with a direct walkway or a meandering garden path. A patio roof, privacy screen, or small fountain can make such a space even more enjoyable.

MULTILEVEL DECKS AND PATIOS. A large lot, especially one with changes in elevation, can often accommodate decks and patios on different levels, linked by steps or

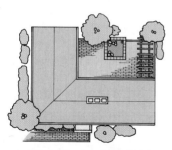

PATIO FOR L-SHAPED HOUSE

WRAPAROUND

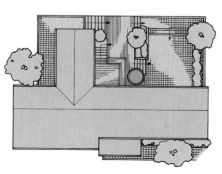

MULTILEVEL LAYOUT

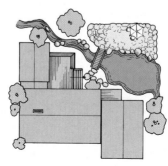

DETACHED PATIO

pathways. Such a scheme works well when your outdoor space must serve many purposes.

ROOFTOP AND BALCONY SITES. No open space in the yard? Look up. A garage rooftop adjacent to a second-story living area might be ideal for a sunny outdoor lounging space. Or consider a small balcony patio with a built-in bench and planter box. Just be sure your existing structure can take the weight of additional wood or masonry (consult an architect or structural engineer), and plan for adequate drainage.

ENTRY PATIOS. Pavings, plantings, and perhaps a trickling fountain enclosed by a privacy wall can transform an ordinary entry path or front lawn into a private oasis. If local codes prohibit building high solid walls, try using a hedge, arbor, or trellis to let in light and air while screening off the street.

SIDE-YARD SPACES. A neglected side yard may be just the spot for a sheltered outdoor sitting area to brighten and expand a small bedroom or master bath. And what about a container-grown herb garden or sunny breakfast deck off a cramped kitchen, accessed by way of French or sliding doors? If you're subject to fence height restrictions, use an arbor or overhead structure to protect privacy.

INTERIOR COURTYARDS. If you're designing a new home, consider incorporating a private interior courtyard, or atrium. If you're remodeling, perhaps your new living space could enclose an existing patio area.

PORCHES. Where summers swelter, the classic porch still evokes a traditional kind of indoor-outdoor living. In bug country, however, screened porches or sunrooms make sense. Some porches can be opened up when the sun shines and battened down when hard winds blow.

RECLAIMED DRIVEWAYS. Your driveway can double as a masonry patio. Concrete turf blocks can support car traffic but yield a softer appearance than plain asphalt or concrete; planting small spaces between pavers achieves the same result. Enclosed by a gate, the front drive becomes an entry courtyard.

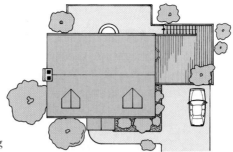

GARAGE ROOFTOP

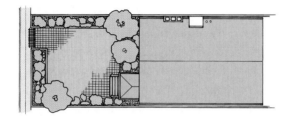

ENTRY PATIO

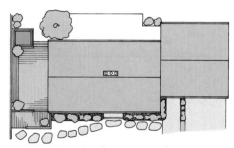

SIDE-YARD SPACE

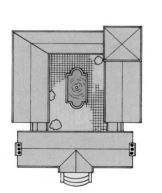

INTERIOR COURTYARD

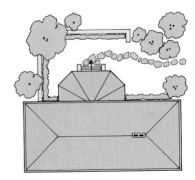

BACK PORCH

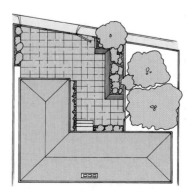

RECLAIMED DRIVEWAY

How's your weather?

Your site's exposure to sun, wind, rain, and snow can limit its potential as an enjoyable outdoor room. Microclimates (weather pockets created by very localized conditions) can also make a big difference. Studying these might prompt you to adjust the site of your proposed deck or patio, extend its dimensions, or change its design. You may be able to moderate the impact of the weather with the addition of an overhead structure, walls, screens, or plantings.

BASIC ORIENTATION. In general, a site that faces north is cold because it receives little sun. A south-facing patio is usually warm because it gets daylong sun. An east-facing patio is likely to be cool, receiving only morning sun. A west-facing patio can be unbearably hot because it gets the full force of the afternoon sun; in late afternoon, it may also fill with harsh glare.

But there are exceptions. For example, since mid-July temperatures in Phoenix often climb

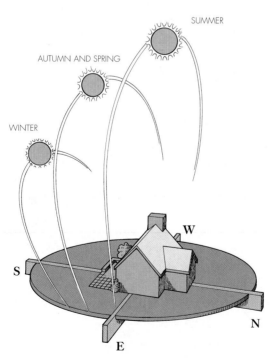

The sun's rays strike your property at predictable angles, depending on the time of year and where you live. A south-facing patio gets maximum sun and heat; a northern site is coldest.

above 100°F, a north-facing patio there could hardly be called "cold." In San Francisco, on the other hand, a patio with a southern or western exposure would not feel overly warm in July because stiff ocean breezes and chilly fogs are common then.

SEASONAL PATHS OF THE SUN. Another factor to consider is the sun's path during the year. As the sun passes over your house, it makes an arc that changes slightly every day, becoming higher in summer and lower in winter. Changes in the sun's path not only give us long days in summer and short ones in winter, but also alter shade patterns in your yard.

UNDERSTANDING WIND. Having too much wind blowing across your patio on a cool day can be just as unpleasant as having no breeze at all on a hot day. Check your lot in relation to three types of air movement: annual prevailing winds, localized seasonal breezes (daily, late-afternoon, or summer), and high-velocity blasts generated by stormy weather.

Chances are that air currents around your house are slightly different from those generally prevailing in your neighborhood. Wind flows like water—after blowing through the trees, it may spill over the house and drop onto your patio. Post small flags or ribbons where you want wind protection and note their movements during windy periods. You'll soon see where you need shelter. If you decide to build a screen or fence to block wind, remember that a solid barrier may not necessarily be the best choice. Sometimes angled baffles, lattice-type fencing, or appropriate plantings disperse wind better.

DEALING WITH RAIN OR SNOW. If, in assessing your climate, you learn that winter storms generally blow out of the northeast, you may want to locate your patio or deck where it will take less of a beating from the weather—perhaps on the south side of the house, where it will be partially protected by trees or a roof overhang.

If you live in an area where brief summer cloudbursts frequently occur, you can extend

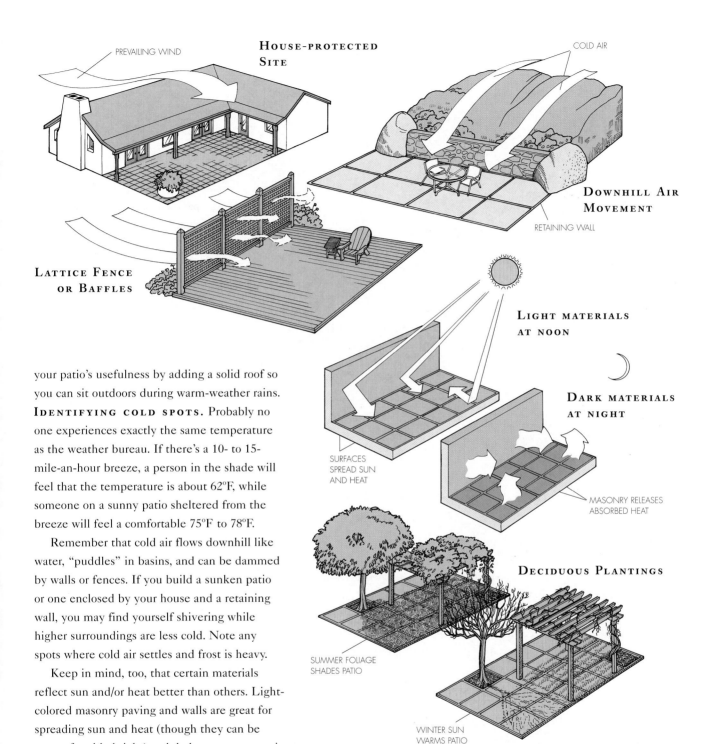

PREVAILING WIND

**HOUSE-PROTECTED
SITE**

COLD AIR

**DOWNHILL AIR
MOVEMENT**

RETAINING WALL

**LATTICE FENCE
OR BAFFLES**

**LIGHT MATERIALS
AT NOON**

**DARK MATERIALS
AT NIGHT**

SURFACES
SPREAD SUN
AND HEAT

MASONRY RELEASES
ABSORBED HEAT

DECIDUOUS PLANTINGS

SUMMER FOLIAGE
SHADES PATIO

WINTER SUN
WARMS PATIO

your patio's usefulness by adding a solid roof so
you can sit outdoors during warm-weather rains.
IDENTIFYING COLD SPOTS. Probably no
one experiences exactly the same temperature
as the weather bureau. If there's a 10- to 15-
mile-an-hour breeze, a person in the shade will
feel that the temperature is about 62°F, while
someone on a sunny patio sheltered from the
breeze will feel a comfortable 75°F to 78°F.

Remember that cold air flows downhill like
water, "puddles" in basins, and can be dammed
by walls or fences. If you build a sunken patio
or one enclosed by your house and a retaining
wall, you may find yourself shivering while
higher surroundings are less cold. Note any
spots where cold air settles and frost is heavy.

Keep in mind, too, that certain materials
reflect sun and/or heat better than others. Light-
colored masonry paving and walls are great for
spreading sun and heat (though they can be
uncomfortably bright) and dark masonry materials retain heat longer, making evenings on the
patio a little warmer. Strategically placed barrier
plantings can help block wind, while allowing
some breezes through. Deciduous trees can
shelter a patio from hot sun in summer, yet
admit welcome rays on crisp winter days, when
their leaves are gone.

*Microclimates affect patio comfort, as shown. Cold air flows
downhill and may be dammed by a house or wall (at top); light-
colored materials reflect light and heat, dark colors absorb it
(center); deciduous plantings provide shade in summer, allow sun
to penetrate in winter (at bottom).*

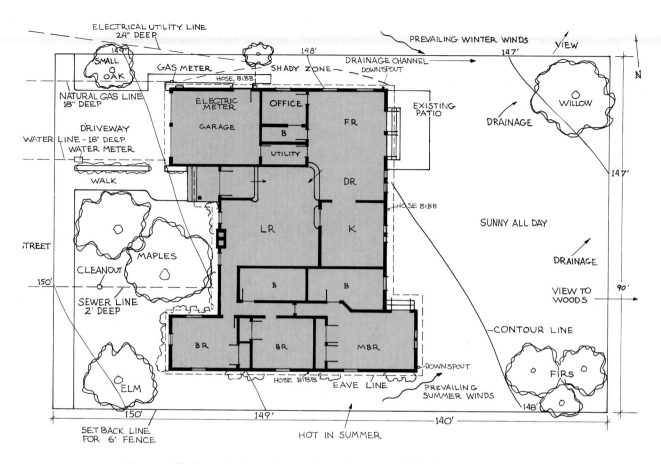

A base map, like the sample shown above, can be one of your most effective planning tools.

Making a base map

Even if you've lived with a landscape for years, mapping it can be a way to make some interesting discoveries about what you thought was familiar territory. Use your observations about your site to produce a base map like the one shown above. Later, slip the base map under tracing paper to sketch designs to your heart's content.

You can save yourself hours of measuring and data-gathering by obtaining dimensions, gradients, and relevant structural details from your deed map, house plans, or a contour map of your lot. If you don't have these, see if they're available through your city hall, county office, title company, bank, or mortgage company.

The following information should appear in one form or another on the base map.

■ **BOUNDARY LINES AND DIMENSIONS.** Outline your property accurately and to scale, and mark its dimensions on the base map. Indicate any required setback allowances from your lot lines. Also note the relation of the street to your house.

■ **THE HOUSE.** Show your house to scale within the property. Note all exterior doors (and the way each one opens), the height of all lower-story windows, and all overhangs. Mark the locations of all downspouts and any drainage tiles, drainpipes, or catch basins.

■ **EXPOSURE.** Draw a north arrow, using a compass; then note on your base map the shaded and sunlit areas of your landscape. Indicate the direction of the prevailing wind and mark any spots that are windy enough to require shielding. Also note any microclimates.

■ **UTILITIES AND EASEMENTS.** Map the placement of hose bibbs and show the locations of all underground lines, including the sewage line or septic tank. If you're contemplating a patio roof or elevated deck, identify any overhead lines.

■ **GRADIENT AND DRAINAGE.** Draw contour lines on your base map, noting high and low points (here's where the official contour map is helpful). If drainage crosses boundaries, you may need to indicate the gradient of adjacent properties as well, to be sure you're not channeling runoff onto your neighbor's property.

Where does the water from paved surfaces drain? Note any point where drainage is impeded (leaving soggy soil) and any place where runoff from a steep hillside could cause erosion.

■ **EXISTING PLANTINGS.** If you're remodeling an old landscape, note any established plantings that you want to retain or that would require a major effort or expense to remove or replace.

■ **VIEWS.** Note all views, attractive or unattractive—the outlook will affect your enjoyment of your patio. If appropriate, you can use a ladder to check views from different elevations. Consider whether a patio, deck, or similar structure might block a favorite view from inside the house. Also take into account views into your yard from nearby houses or streets.

Code concerns

Before you launch into the design phase, check with your local building department to find out whether you need a building permit and learn what codes affect a potential structure's design and placement. Local codes and ordinances can govern the height of an outdoor structure, its maximum footprint, the materials from which it is built, its setback from lot lines, and even the nailing pattern its construction requires.

Also check your property deed for possible building easements or restrictions that might affect your project's location or design. Note any relevant code concerns on your base map.

TOOLS OF THE TRADE

To draw your base map (and, later, your final plan), you'll need 24- by 36-inch graph paper (¼-inch scale, unless the size of your property requires ⅛-inch scale), an art gum eraser, a straightedge, several pencils, and a pad of tracing paper. Optional are a drafting board, a T-square, one or more triangles, a compass, a circle template, and an architect's scale. For taking measurements in the existing landscape, choose either a 50- or 100-foot tape measure; anything shorter is exasperating to use and can lead to inaccurate measurements.

You can draw your base map directly on graph paper or on tracing paper placed over graph paper. (If you plan to have a blueprinting company make copies of your base map, you will have to use tracing paper; a blueprint machine will not accept regular graph paper.)

If you can use a personal computer, don't overlook the growing collection of drawing and landscape-planning software programs. Unlike earlier CAD programs aimed at professionals, some of the newer offerings are designed for the more limited skill levels and budgets of homeowners.

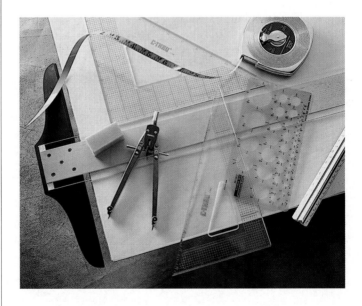

Simple drawing and measuring tools can help produce a clear, easy-to-read base map and final plan. Shown are T-square, 45° and 60° triangles, compass, circle template, eraser, architect's scale, and 50-foot tape measure.

a planning primer

experimenting
with your ideas

WITH YOUR *base map complete, you can begin trying out your ideas and determining the style of your patio or deck. As you brainstorm, you'll begin to work out use areas and circulation patterns and make general decisions about what kinds of structures and amenities you'll need and where to place them. You may also wish to review some design basics (see page 16).*

What's your style?

A Moroccan-tiled water feature sits in a patio of Saltillo pavers; it doubles as both soothing spa and garden pool.

One early design decision you must make is whether you want a formal or informal outdoor environment. The style you choose should be compatible with the architecture of your house and appropriate to your climate.

Formal landscapes are symmetrical, with straight lines, geometric patterns, and clearly established balance; they often include sheared hedges, topiaries, and fountains, pools, or outdoor sculpture. Paving might be of mortared brick, cut stone, tile, or poured concrete.

Informal styles, on the other hand, tend to favor curves, asymmetry, and apparent randomness; adjacent plantings are usually more naturalistic, too. Masonry units, if used, are set in more casual sand beds (see page 21). Flagstones, river rocks, and gravel can give a native, nature-oriented look. Wooden decks seem at home in just about any informal setting.

You can learn a lot about style by studying gardens that you visit or see in magazines, as well as those illustrated throughout this book. Here are some stylistic themes that are part of a wide range you may encounter:

- Period (as in Georgian, Victorian)
- Mediterranean
- Tropical
- Asian
- Avant-garde
- Rustic
- Naturalistic
- Eclectic

Patio styles traverse a spectrum from rustic through eclectic. The one above features spaced stepping-stones and mortared twin "islands" of Arizona flagstone that fit with a nearly natural background of gravel, ground covers, border plantings, and mature oaks. The patio at left uses diagonally laid slate tiles to set off sculptural palms, a planting of tall horsetails, and whimsically colorful furniture.

GUIDES TO GOOD DESIGN

Experienced landscape professionals employ several criteria to ensure that a deck or patio is useful and comfortable and that it also complements its surroundings visually. In well-designed landscapes no one plant, structure, or feature stands out too much, but rather all the parts work together to establish a sense of unity. Note how construction materials or plants are used with repetition or placed for dramatic emphasis. All the elements should be in proportion to the rest of the garden and in scale with the size of the house, the property, and the people who live there. Also, note how harmony is achieved by balancing simplicity (in form, texture, and color) and variety (in materials and plants).

When planning, you may also wish to review the following specifics.

■ **Meet your needs.** Your design should be able to accommodate your family's favorite activities, from relaxation and casual gatherings to children's games, barbecues, and entertaining.

■ **Protect privacy.** As an extension of your indoor living space, your patio should offer the same feeling of privacy as interior rooms do, but with no sense of confinement. Building an elevated deck, for example, can open as many unpleasant views as attractive ones—and expose you to view as well. Do you need to add screens, arbors, or plantings to remedy the problem? Could an ivy-draped wall and a trickling fountain help buffer unwanted noise?

This private side-yard sitting area, paved with widely spaced flagstones, marks a gentle transition between a formal brick landing and the nearby rose garden.

■ **Be aware of safety.** Patio paving materials have different properties. For example, some become slippery when wet; others are too sharp or uneven for children's games. Passage from house to patio and from deck to garden must be safe and unobstructed. Adequate lighting should be provided at steps and along garden paths.

■ **Use color.** As in a beautiful indoor room, colors should be placed in a coordinated relationship to one another. Brick, adobe, wood, and stone have distinctive, generally earthy colors. Concrete has more industrial overtones, but can be softened with aggregate, stamping and staining, or integral color.

Even plants on or around your patio or deck should contribute harmonious tones. Use complementary colors sparingly, as accents. Remember that all foliage is not simply "green"; the range of shades is really very large.

■ **Think transitions.** A patio or deck should entice people outdoors. So be sure to consider the transition from the inside of your house to the outside. Wide French or sliding glass doors make the outdoors look inviting and also make the interior space expand psychologically.

Try to create attractive transitions between different areas of the deck or patio and between these and the rest of the garden. The use of edgings, borders, steps, and railings can make or break your design.

Define use areas

Focus on your family's needs and activities. Think about the way you live, making a list of what's most important to you (if you have children, get their input, too); then, if you need to compromise, you can compromise on the less important things.

Next, review your yard's assets. Can your plan capitalize on a fine view? Perhaps your design can take advantage of a sunny southern exposure or an impressive garden tree.

Consider also your yard's handicaps. Is your lot on a steep slope? How much of the lot is exposed to street noise or a neighbor's view? If you're rethinking an existing patio or deck, ask yourself whether it opens off the wrong room, gets too much sun or shade, or lacks sufficient space.

Now get ready to try out your ideas. For each design attempt, use a separate sheet of tracing paper placed over your base map, sketching rough circular or oval shapes ("balloons") to represent the location and approximate size of each use area. For an example, see the drawing at right.

As you sketch, concentrate on logical placement and juxtaposition. Are you locating a children's play area in full view of your living area? Is the small, private sunning spot you envision easily accessible from the master bedroom? Do you really want a patio designed for entertaining guests to be located next to the recycling bins? If you have doubts about the lay of the land, consult the information on grading and drainage on page 22.

Design with shapes

When your experiments with diagrams have resulted in a rough sketch, lay a clean sheet of tracing paper on top of it. On this sheet, and on as many more as you need, begin drawing in the various building blocks of the design—paving, enclosing walls or hedges, arbors, benches, and perhaps a pool or spa.

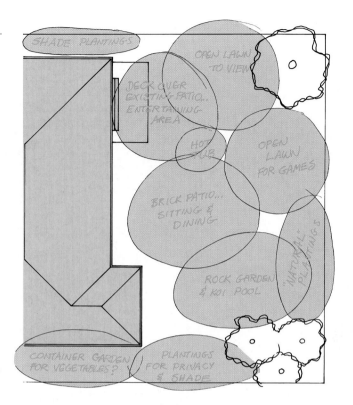

To make a balloon sketch, place tracing paper over your base map; then sketch circles to indicate use areas and other features. Keep circulation patterns in mind. Consider your design as a whole, balancing design elements and relating the patio to both garden and house. Draw as many designs as you can—early mistakes cost nothing.

At this point, keep in mind two tricks of the landscape designer. First, work with clear, simple shapes; second, relate those shapes to the lines of your house. A design that is made up of familiar shapes such as squares, rectangles, triangles, and circles is easier to understand than one filled with abstract lines. Repeating a familiar shape brings simplicity and order to the design, unifying paving, paths, walls, arbors, and other features.

To add interest, vary the sizes of the shapes you work with, but don't use too many little shapes or you will end up with a very busy design. Add a curve, perhaps, to connect two rectangular spaces, or use a diagonal line to emphasize the longest dimension in a small gar-

CLEARANCE FOR TABLE WITH CHAIRS

RISING SPACE 32"

SIDE PASSAGE 22"
(32" FOR HANDICAPPED)

PATHWAY CLEARANCE

4' TO 5'

2' TO 3'

SERVICE PATHWAY

MAIN PATHWAY

BENCH CLEARANCE

3'   3'

SITTING   WALKING

A PLANNING CHECKLIST

Look closely at the successful deck and patio designs shown in "Great Patios and Decks," pages 26–89. What components do you need to include to create your own ideal outdoor environment? Which materials would work best in your situation? (For practical guidance, also look through the information in "A Shopper's Guide," pages 91–109.)

As you begin to firm up your design, account for the following structural elements:

- Decking or paving materials
- Retaining wall for hilly or sloping areas
- Walls, fences, or screens for privacy or noise control
- Overhead structures
- Steps or formal stairs for changes in level
- Walks and footpaths linking use areas
- Edgings where appropriate
- French or sliding door for access from the house

Although some finishing touches, such as outdoor benches and planters, can be added later, now is the best time to think about the amenities you want and to sketch them on your design. If you might want to add lighting or perhaps a sink or wet bar to your outdoor living area later, plan now for the necessary wire or pipe runs.

- Arbor or trellis
- Gazebo
- Garden pool, fountain, waterfall, or stream
- Spa or hot tub
- Barbecue area or kitchen facilities
- Storage cabinets or shelves
- Built-in benches or other furniture
- Outdoor lighting (120-volt or low-voltage)
- GFCI-protected electrical outlets
- Outdoor heater or fireplace
- Hose bibb
- Raised beds for plants or built-in planter, perhaps with built-in drip irrigation

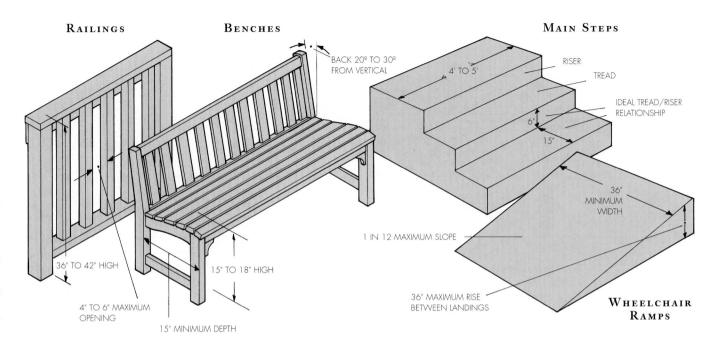

RAILINGS

BENCHES

MAIN STEPS

BACK 20º TO 30º FROM VERTICAL

RISER

TREAD

4' TO 5'

IDEAL TREAD/RISER RELATIONSHIP

6"

15"

36" TO 42" HIGH

15" TO 18" HIGH

4" TO 6" MAXIMUM OPENING

15" MINIMUM DEPTH

36" MINIMUM WIDTH

1 IN 12 MAXIMUM SLOPE

36" MAXIMUM RISE BETWEEN LANDINGS

WHEELCHAIR RAMPS

den. Some structures will work themselves very naturally into your plan and others won't fit at all. Use the checklist on the facing page to help select the features that will serve your situation best.

Examine circulation patterns

Also consider foot-traffic connections between use areas, as well as from individual areas to the house and yard. Will too much traffic be channeled through areas meant for relaxation? Can guests move easily from the entertainment area to the garden? Can the lawn mower or garden cart be moved from the toolshed to the lawn without disturbing someone's repose?

One way to improve access to and from the house is to add a door. But if you have to open up a wall to improve circulation, be sure you won't end up producing a traffic pattern that runs through the middle of a room.

When planning pathways, steps, and other parts of the route, you'll need to allow at least the established minimum clearances; for guidelines, see the illustrations above and on the facing page.

MAKING A MOCK-UP

If you are having difficulty visualizing the finished landscape or can't quite decide on the specifics of certain elements, you may wish to mock up the design on your actual property. Seeing an approximation of the layout in the form of stakes, strings, and other markings can help you determine the exact dimensions necessary for features such as decks, terraces, and walks.

To outline paving areas, patio or deck construction, pathways, and planting beds with straight or gently curved lines, mark each corner with a short stake and connect the stakes with string. Use taller stakes to mark fences and walls. Tall stakes can also represent trees or elements like fountains, sculptures, or posts for overhead construction.

If your design is mostly curves and free-form shapes, snake a garden hose to lay out the lines to your liking. Limestone or gypsum, common soil amendments, can be used to lay out freeform designs such as the outlines of planting beds and borders. Powdered chalk in different colors is useful if you have overlapping elements. To revise your plan, simply turn the powder over into the soil and start again.

nuts and bolts

WHETHER OR NOT *you intend to build your patio or deck yourself, you'll want a basic understanding of the materials and methods involved. A knowledge of these details can help you evaluate your do-it-yourself zeal and zero in on material costs; you'll also be able to communicate more easily with dealers and professionals.*

Patio profiles

Most patios are constructed in one of two ways—with a poured concrete slab or base or atop a bed of clean, packed sand.

A concrete slab suits heavy-use areas and formal designs. The slab should be at least 4 inches thick (see drawing on facing page, top) and, for better drainage, underlaid with 2 to 8 inches of gravel. Welded wire mesh helps reinforce the structure. Wooden forms define the slab's shape; they're usually removed once the concrete has set. Wet concrete is poured into the forms like batter into a cake pan. While still plastic, the concrete is leveled and the surface is smoothed. Colored aggregates (small stones) or stamped patterns can customize and soften the concrete's appearance.

A thinner concrete pad, typically about 3 inches thick, can serve as the base for masonry units such as ceramic tile or flagstones set in mortar (see drawing on facing page, bottom).

A sand bed (see drawing on facing page, center) is popular for casual brick, paver, and cobblestone patios and walks, and some contractors use this method for formal work, too. A layer of gravel provides drainage and stability; damp sand is then carefully leveled—or "screeded"—on top. Paving units, either spaced or tightly butted, go atop the screeded bed, and then additional sand is cast over the surface and worked into joints to lock units in place. Edgings help define the patio and keep units from shifting.

Whatever surface you choose, you should slope it a minimum of 1 inch per 8 feet for drainage. Walkways can be angled slightly so that water is channeled away.

Deck details

If grade or drainage presents insurmountable problems, or if you simply prefer the look and feel of a wooden surface, a deck may be your choice.

A deck can be freestanding or, as shown on page 23, attached to the house via a horizontal ledger. The structure is designed with a stacking principle in mind, with each new layer perpendicular to the one below. Concrete footings secure precast piers or poured, tubular pads, which in turn support vertical wooden posts. Horizontal beams span the posts; joists run perpendicular to ledger and beams. The

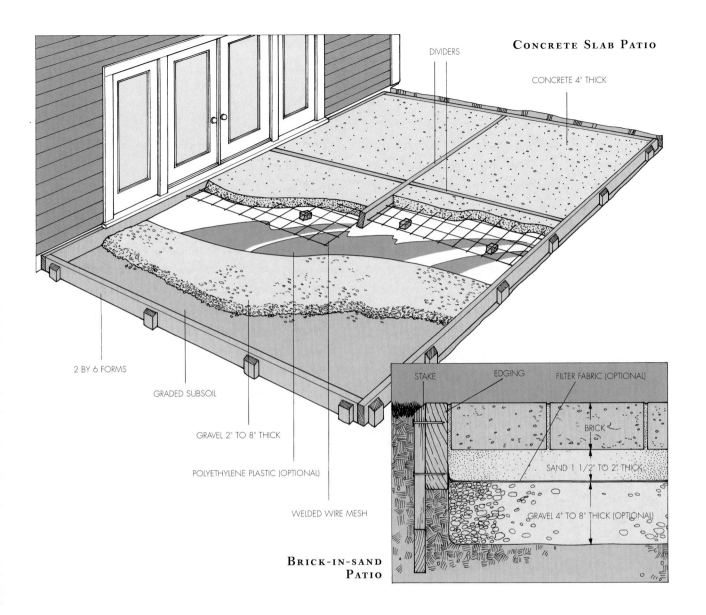

CONCRETE SLAB PATIO

DIVIDERS

CONCRETE 4" THICK

2 BY 6 FORMS

GRADED SUBSOIL

GRAVEL 2" TO 8" THICK

POLYETHYLENE PLASTIC (OPTIONAL)

WELDED WIRE MESH

BRICK-IN-SAND PATIO

STAKE

EDGING

FILTER FABRIC (OPTIONAL)

BRICK

SAND 1 1/2" TO 2" THICK

GRAVEL 4" TO 8" THICK (OPTIONAL)

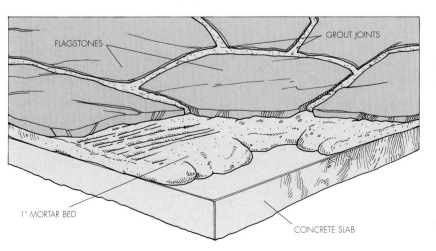

FLAGSTONES

GROUT JOINTS

FLAGSTONES IN MORTAR

1" MORTAR BED

CONCRETE SLAB

OBSERVING THE LAY OF THE LAND

Whenever you can fit any landscape element into the existing topography with little or no disturbance of the soil, you save time, effort, and expense.

However, that isn't always possible. Sometimes the existing topography has inherent problems, or you realize you must alter it in order to accommodate your ideal design. Then you must grade the site—reshape it by removing soil, adding soil, or both. In most cases, it's best to consult a landscape architect or soils engineer.

If your property lies on a slope so steep that without skillful grading and terracing it would remain unstable and useless, consider constructing one or a series of retaining walls. The safest way to build a retaining wall is to place it at the bottom of a gentle slope, if space permits, and fill in behind it. That way you won't disturb the stability of the soil. Otherwise, the hill can be held either with a single high wall or with a series of low walls forming graceful terraces.

Always route water away from the house. If your landscape is nearly flat, it must have adequate surface drainage—a minimum slope of 1 inch per 8 feet of paved surface, or nearly 3 inches per 10 feet of unpaved ground. Steeper gradients are better for slow-draining, heavy soils.

Where property slopes toward the house, you may need to shore it up with a retaining wall and slope surfaces to direct runoff to a central drain, like a "bathtub."

Poor subsurface drainage can be a problem where the water table is close to the surface. Plastic drainpipes or dry wells can be the answer in many situations. But a major problem calls for a sump pump. To plan and install a drainage system for a problem hillside, get professional help.

STANDARD SLOPED RUNOFF

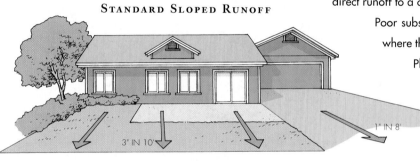

3" IN 10'   1" IN 8'

A uniform slope, as shown above, directs water away from the house; hilly yards and retaining walls may call for a central catch basin, as shown below.

"BATHTUB" PATIO

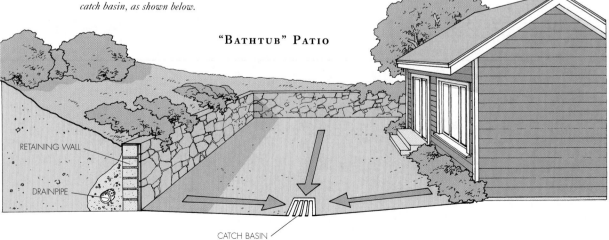

RETAINING WALL

DRAINPIPE

CATCH BASIN

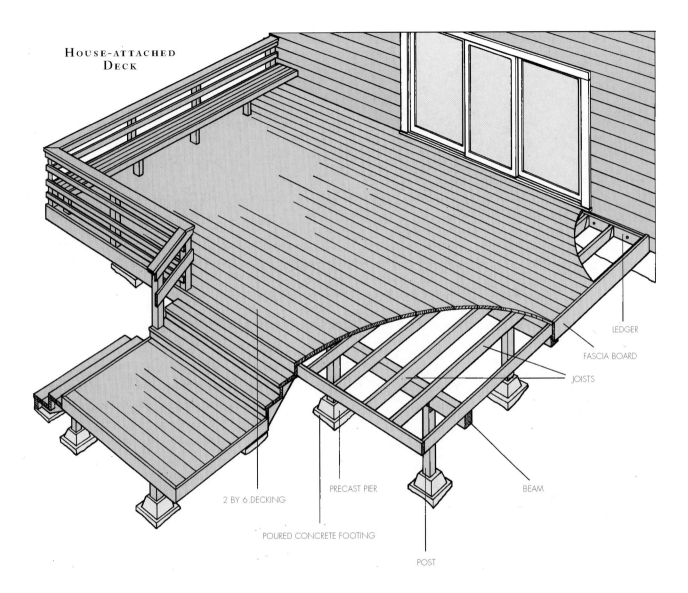

HOUSE-ATTACHED
DECK

LEDGER

FASCIA BOARD

JOISTS

BEAM

POST

PRECAST PIER

2 BY 6 DECKING

POURED CONCRETE FOOTING

decking itself, typically 2 by 4 or 2 by 6 lumber, is nailed or screwed to the joists. Be sure that your decking is at least 1 inch below any door sill and that there are ⅛- to ³⁄₁₆-inch drainage gaps between boards.

Overhead structures, benches, railings, and steps are often integral to a deck's framing. While it may be feasible to add these later, it's simplest to design and build the whole project at once.

In a deck's structure, the size and spacing of each component affect the members above and below. Minimum and maximum sizes are stipulated by your building code. Posts taller than about 3 feet may require bracing, especially in areas prone to earthquakes or high winds. Elevated decks require railings (again, specified by local code).

Fascia boards, skirts, and other trim details help add a custom touch to the basic structure. For a closer look at decking lumber, hardware, and finishes, see "A Shopper's Guide," pages 91–109.

Are you planning a rooftop deck? It must be sloped above an impermeable membrane—a job for a roofing contractor.

gearing up

O NCE YOU'VE DECIDED *how you want to use your outdoor space, what type of structure will accomplish this best, and what alterations of gradient are called for, you're ready to firm up your plan. This rendering is the end result of the design process; use it for fine-tuning, for estimating materials, and when talking with professionals.*

The final plan

To create your plan, place a sheet of tracing paper over your base map. Draw carefully and label all features clearly. Most designers create a "plan" view and one or more "elevations." (A plan view is the classic bird's-eye view of the layout as if seen from above; an elevation, or straight-on view, shows how the scene would look to a person standing in one spot nearby.) If

What's your choice— earthy and muted, or sleekly smooth? Classic masonry units, like the terra-cotta tiles and green-glazed accents shown at right, fit well in many regional and traditional settings. But the cast-concrete veranda on the facing page makes a sophisticated, modern statement, spreading down past concentric steps from a sheltered entertainment patio with built-in barbecue and fireplace.

you have a knack for design, there's no reason why you can't develop a working plan, though it's wise to have at least an hour's consultation with a professional landscape architect or designer (see facing page).

Can you do it yourself?

If you are a skilled weekend carpenter, you should have no serious problem building a simple deck or overhead structure, such as an arbor. However, certain conditions may require professional help.

A deck on unstable soil, sand, mud, or water needs special foundations for support—and perhaps the advice of an engineer as well as of a builder. A high-level deck or one on a steep hillside also involves special design methods and may be too difficult for an amateur to build.

Concrete work, while straightforward, can present a logistical and physical challenge. If your job is complex or requires a large, continuous pour, leave it to pros. Patios assembled from smaller units such as bricks or stones can be built at a more leisurely pace. But be advised that, for the average weekend mason, the constant lifting, mixing, and shoveling may take their toll.

Working with professionals

Who is the right advisor to help you adapt, develop, or build your patio or deck? Here are some of the people who can offer assistance, along with a brief look at what they do.

ARCHITECTS AND LANDSCAPE ARCHITECTS. These state-licensed professionals have a bachelor's or master's degree in architecture or landscape architecture. They're trained to create designs that are structurally sound, functional, and esthetically pleasing. They know construction materials, can negotiate bids from contractors, and can supervise the actual work. Many are willing to give a simple consultation, either in their offices or at your home, for a modest fee.

LANDSCAPE AND BUILDING DESIGNERS. Landscape designers usually have a landscape architect's education and training but not a state license. Building designers, whether licensed (by the American Institute of Building Designers) or unlicensed, may offer design help along with construction services.

DRAFTSPERSONS. Drafters may be members of a skilled trade or unlicensed architects' apprentices. They can make the working drawings (from which you or your contractor can work) needed for building permits.

STRUCTURAL AND SOILS ENGINEERS. If you're planning to build a structure on an unstable or steep lot or where heavy wind or loads come into play, you should consult an engineer.

A soils engineer evaluates soil conditions and establishes design specifications for foundations. A structural engineer, often working with the calculations a soils engineer provides, designs foundation piers and footings to suit the site. Engineers also provide wind- and load-stress calculations as required.

GENERAL AND LANDSCAPE CONTRACTORS. Licensed general and landscape contractors specialize in construction (landscape contractors specialize in garden construction), though some have design experience as well. They usually charge less for design work than landscape architects do, but their skills may be limited by a construction point of view.

Contractors may do the work themselves or assume responsibility for ordering materials, hiring qualified subcontractors, and seeing that the job is completed according to contract.

SUBCONTRACTORS. If you prefer to act as your own general contractor, it's up to you to hire, coordinate, and supervise whatever subcontractors the job requires—specialists in carpentry, grading, and the like. Aside from doing the work according to your drawings, subcontractors can often supply you with product information and procure materials. Of course, you can hire other workers on your own; but in that case, you'll be responsible for permits, insurance, and any payroll taxes.

GREAT PATIOS AND DECKS

IF YOU'RE LOOKING for inspiration, you've come to the right place. The following pages are crammed with photos that showcase both patios and decks in action. You'll find a wide range of materials, formal and informal styles, landscapes large and small. **WE BEGIN** with two large sections that traverse a range of successful patio and deck designs. Then come sections with outstanding solutions to some common—and not so common—site problems. **AS YOU BROWSE,** note the custom touches that turn a basic platform into a distinctive outdoor room. Pay particular attention to edgings and borders; as pros know, these transitions can make or break your design. Feel free to borrow a deck detail here, a patio accent there. Many of these ideas are appropriate for either wood or masonry, or for a mix of both. **IF AVAILABILITY** is a question, you'll find plenty of information on specific materials in "A Shopper's Guide," beginning on page 91.

patio profiles

MANY PATIO STYLES are established, at least in part, by the materials you choose for them. Brick is one of the most adaptable and frequently used surfaces available. Set in mortar or, more casually, in sand, brick can blend with nearly any architectural or landscaping style. Precast concrete pavers, available in many shapes and sizes, can be used in much the same way as brick—in fact, in some areas, "brick-style" pavers are more popular than the real thing.

Though often typecast as cold and forbidding, poured concrete is perhaps even more adaptable than brick. Used with the proper forms and reinforcement, it can conform to almost any shape. It can be lightly smoothed or heavily brushed, surfaced with colorful pebbles, swirled, scored, tinted, patterned, or molded to resemble another material.

Ceramic tile works well in both formal and informal situations. From the earthy tones of terra-cotta to the bright primaries of hand-painted accents, tile can support just about any landscaping style. Flat flagstones and cut stone tiles are ideal for formal paving. For a more informal look, you can use more irregularly shaped rocks and pebbles, setting them in soil or embedding them in concrete.

For economy, good drainage, and a more casual look, consider including loose materials such as pea gravel, bark, or wood chips in your patio plan. Gravel can be raked into patterns or used as a decorative filler with other materials. You might employ dividers to set off different colors and textures.

Seeded aggregate creates a classic, nonskid concrete surface. An octagonal brick border defines the dining area; matching brickwork is used in other parts of the patio.

Tile leftovers, colored stones, and a set of concrete footprints form a whorled and whimsical courtyard mosaic.

*An outdoor room with a crackling fire makes the day's
warmth linger longer. The brick patio, set in a classic
running-bond pattern, surrounds a small pond and gentle
waterfall. Low walls with flagstone caps corral plantings
and provide extra seating.*

This rear patio's formal brickwork is set on concrete with neatly tooled mortar joints, continuing the orderly look of the stucco-clad two-story house behind.

A geometric pattern of concrete pavers tops an easy-draining base of filter fabric and packed gravel. Pressure-treated wooden edgings help lock the patio in place.

A blue concrete river meanders through a side-yard patio, past fragmented islands in a gray field. A band of dark blue ceramic tile halts the flow of curves. Some areas of concrete are smooth, others scored and brushed.

The outdoor sitting area above features alternating patches of Korean grass and spaced concrete paver blocks that support the casual furniture. Young crab apple trees follow the curving boundary between patio and garden.

A sunny wraparound veranda is clothed in nonslip, light-toned concrete that stays cool in direct sun. Note how the concrete's color and texture complement the house's exterior walls.

Patinaed by time, this Mediterranean-style courtyard blends terra-cotta tile squares and diagonally set blue-glazed accents. The design centers on a vibrant tiled fountain.

There's no law against having fun with tile. Colorful Malibu tiles, shown above, make lively porch accents. The playful path shown at right sports custom-painted, randomly placed striped tile squares.

Slick tiles can be trouble outdoors, but some new glazed floor tiles are toothy enough for safe footing on the veranda. And while they resemble both stone and terra-cotta, they're easier to maintain than either.

*At once formal and earthy, these Indian slate tiles, with
matching accent courses, help wrap an outdoor pavilion
and adjacent pool in warm, variegated tones.*

Arizona flagstone slabs are laid with tight joints; some are grouted, but many cracks remain, allowing lemon thyme and woolly thyme to gain a footing.

A colorful mosaic compass stands out against background pavement of randomly shaped broken flagstones.

A front-yard clearing, lined with gray gravel and ringed

by old stone walls and colorful flower beds, forms a

casual and comfortable backdrop for dining, gardening,

or—in the orange cat's case—some serious snoozing.

Gravel's casual appeal makes an effective transition from formal patio to the garden proper. Here, graveled areas are bounded by curved rubber edgings for a striking contrast in color and texture.

This highly sculptured study in dark pea gravel and vanilla-colored concrete is broken by a poured concrete bench and curb and by planting beds strewn with red-wood chips.

great patios and decks

decked out

FEW MATERIALS can match the natural, informal quality of wood. Its warm color and soft texture bring something of the forest into your landscape, and if stained or painted, wood can hold its own in even the most formal company.

A wooden deck—either freestanding or house-attached—provides a solid, relatively durable surface requiring little or no grading and a minimum of maintenance. Because decking is raised above the ground and can dry quickly, it's a natural wherever drainage is a problem.

For even less maintenance and a lower environmental impact, consider surface decking that's made from recycled materials; a graphic example is shown on the facing page. (Note, however, that you'll still need wood or another material for structural members; this decking is not rated for strength.)

Whether it's new or old, natural or man-made, decking at ground level feels right in almost any outdoor setting. A low-lying deck can link house and garden at flower-head height, smoothing out bumps and riding over drainage problems that might preclude masonry pavings. A wrap-around extends living space into the landscape, offering an unbeatable way to expand cramped living quarters.

Any deck more than 30 inches above the ground requires a railing or similar barrier. Beyond safety, railings contribute an important design element, too. What's the view? Use railings to frame it or block it. Fill gaps with vertical slats, safety glass, or screening.

Sunlight glows on a cedar-surfaced waterfront deck; stone slab steps link it to a concrete patio above. Note how the deck's edge is cut to accommodate the big boulders.

This broad backyard structure is at home with the surrounding forest, but its decking "boards" aren't wood—they're splinterless, composite products made largely from recycled plastic. Built-in wooden bench seating surrounds a fire pit that, when covered, becomes a coffee table.

*Natural wood decking
extends the old
concrete slab at house
level; openings make
way for mature oaks,
which double as ham-
mock supports. The
deck is shored up by a
stone-capped retaining
wall; steps lead down
to the paver patio.*

*A low-level cedar deck
seemingly floats above a rock-
lined garden pool; 2 by 3
decking boards are finished with
semi-transparent stain.*

Designed and built by the homeowners and a contractor friend, this house-attached structure features dark-stained 2 by 4 cedar decking with a penetrating finish on top. Built-in benches, planters, and a ground-level "bridge" over river rocks add a note of permanence and help tie the deck to the landscape. So does the deck's skirt, which repeats the house's siding style and color.

A soothing hot tub holds center stage on this detached garden platform. Note the crafted patterns and accents on the deck surface.

This low entry deck establishes a transition between the house and the landscape while providing a smooth surface and efficient drainage. Leisurely curves lead the eye toward the front archway beyond.

Cantilevered above a steep hillside and accessed via a winding "mountain path," this austere perch hovers above a seemingly wild landscape. The deck is sparingly dressed with a space-frame arbor and built-in bench.

A cascade of stairs and landings pinwheels around a rocky outcrop and two venerable trees. The stairs leading from the upper-level deck are freestanding. They're supported by cross-stacked redwood 4 by 4s that allow the curving form to be developed.

Built for entertaining large crowds and guarded by a copper pipe railing, the star of this elegantly planned two-level redwood deck is the built-in sofa in the center. The edge of the upper deck forms the seat; the planter provides back support.

These three decks rail against convention. Child-safe netting, shown above, snaps into place, and can be removed for views or when entertaining. Armed with a saber saw, the owner of the deck shown at top right gave each 1¹/4 by 4-inch cedar rail a whimsical shape. Custom baked-enamel steel railings at right combine with steel cable and turnbuckles for a clean, uncluttered look.

Some views can take your breath away. To keep this one unobstructed while adding wind protection, the owner placed panels of safety glass in the deck railing's straight sections.

coping with slopes

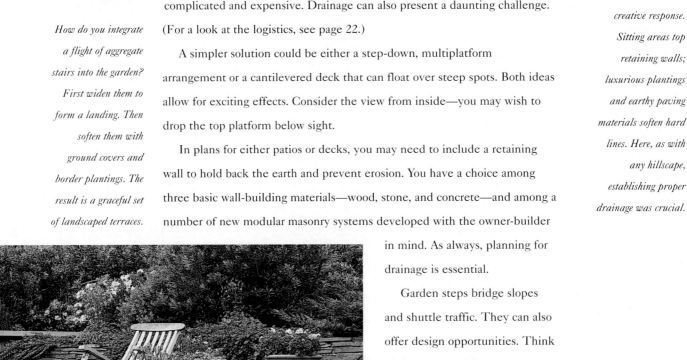

How do you integrate a flight of aggregate stairs into the garden? First widen them to form a landing. Then soften them with ground covers and border plantings. The result is a graceful set of landscaped terraces.

IF YOU'RE FACED with a hilly, hard-to-drain site, you can either learn to live with it or, depending on your soil and your budget, you can start over. Sites that require extensive grading—via excavation and backfilling—can get both complicated and expensive. Drainage can also present a daunting challenge. (For a look at the logistics, see page 22.)

A simpler solution could be either a step-down, multiplatform arrangement or a cantilevered deck that can float over steep spots. Both ideas allow for exciting effects. Consider the view from inside—you may wish to drop the top platform below sight.

In plans for either patios or decks, you may need to include a retaining wall to hold back the earth and prevent erosion. You have a choice among three basic wall-building materials—wood, stone, and concrete—and among a number of new modular masonry systems developed with the owner-builder in mind. As always, planning for drainage is essential.

Garden steps bridge slopes and shuttle traffic. They can also offer design opportunities. Think of them as transition zones between patio levels; extensions might double as benches, planters, or display perches. Regardless of the material you use, put safety first: treads should give safe footing in wet weather, and adequate lighting must be provided. Be sure that step dimensions are comfortable—not too long and not too steep.

A cramped, steep lot presented a design challenge, but this multilevel, multiuse structure was a creative response. Sitting areas top retaining walls; luxurious plantings and earthy paving materials soften hard lines. Here, as with any hillscape, establishing proper drainage was crucial.

A striking multilevel redwood deck glows with warm sunset light. Its layout transforms a steep hillside into a spacious, flexible outdoor room. Built-in benches, wide steps, and matching railings add finishing touches.

What can you do with a steep slope on a small urban lot? This designer built up the slope to make space for a front-yard patio with great views. A new concrete-block retaining wall (right) atop the old one raised its level. The resulting back-filled platform is dressed with concrete pavers, trellised railings, built-in benches, and a sunny garden bed (below).

great patios and decks

small miracles

WHEN SPACE IS SHORT, your landscape must work harder. Vertical stacking is one way to handle sloped or multistory layouts; intensify the available space by creating small, separate areas. For example, let a small elevated deck feed down to a ground-level container-plant patio and onward to a separate sitting area along the back fence. Flat lots also benefit from changes in level—even a few inches.

Small-space designs often employ a deliberate sense of "misdirection." Use diagonal lines and offset patterns to lead the eye outward. Use winding paths, grouped containers, screens, arbors, and plantings to slow traffic, to frame tiny views, and to create hidden spots that blur boundaries. Even the smallest pond or pool can make a space seem larger by creating an illusion of depth and by reflecting the sky and surrounding surfaces.

Invest in quality materials. Pay particular attention to your use of paving and amenities. Because the space is small, it must stand up to close scrutiny.

Consider the inside-outside connection (for ideas, see pages 62–65). A set of glazed doors or a window wall can link the house and garden, stretching space in both directions.

To protect privacy, grow a screen of green. Tall plants or vine-covered arbors block out views of neighboring houses. A trickling waterfall or fountain masks noise.

A hilly, narrow side yard now accommodates a waterfall, a spa, and several sitting areas (one is shown)—all artfully integrated as a series of descending tiers.

A tract lot that was formerly bare dirt now sports whitewashed, low-level decking that's angled to enhance the sense of space. Wood gives way to Saltillo tiles beyond, also laid diagonally. A trickling wall fountain makes a tranquil focal point off the living room. Tall plantings and a house-attached arbor offer a sense of enclosure and screen off the neighbors' houses.

On a steep lot along a busy street, a slender, 12- by 35-foot courtyard leads to this house's

entry. French doors connect the living room directly to the stamped-concrete patio, making

it possible for interior and exterior rooms to borrow space from each other.

A waterfall masks street noise.

A small mixed-gravel patio tucks into the U shape formed by the house and the neighbors' wall at right (not shown). The casual hardscape incorporates both patio and garden, trimming down the more usual space-consuming borders between them. Banks of French doors and windows open to the area, extending interior space, too.

Water makes this narrow urban yard into a small oasis. The waterfall makes a peaceful background sound, while a set of "floating" stepping stones involves inhabitants directly with the landscape.

up-front ideas

WITH LOT SIZES shrinking and land values soaring, you want to make every inch of your outdoor space count. And though we tend to picture the patio area as being behind the house, why not look out front?

In place of lawn and landscaping designed for public view (and not much else), enclose the space with garden walls to create a private front courtyard—a very old Moorish and Spanish tradition. With garden walls in place, you can open up street-facing rooms with a glass door or curtainless windows, bringing in more daylight and playing up the courtyard connection. An arbor overhead adds shade and shelter. You can also move the indoors out, adding amenities such as a fireplace, soft lighting, and a dining area.

Of course, on lots blessed with privacy out in front, you can choose just about any scheme—perhaps adding a knee wall, a screen, or an arbor to help define the space.

A patio might as well start right at the front steps. This set combines flagstone treads and glazed-tile risers. The way leads through a rustic gate to a raised front patio of spaced flagstones with grass growing between them.

Twin arched arbors frame the brick path from the street to a front-yard patio just beyond the swinging teak privacy doors. The house entry is to the left past the doors.

Driveways can do double duty. Soften harsh paving with planting pockets or replace it with concrete turf blocks. Relegate the car to its allotted corner and reclaim the remainder as a courtyard. Good-looking interlocking pavers say "patio," but can stand up to car traffic.

A front-yard room may be simpler to build than an indoor room of comparable size, but it is still subject to building codes. Of primary concern are the wall height and the setback from the street.

An inviting private courtyard (right) has a pitch-roofed
arbor overhead, rising above the curve of the arched entry-
way. The space enjoys morning sunlight, but thanks to the
fireplace, it's also suitable for evening entertaining. The
new front wall (above) recaptures part of the driveway.

Cantilevered over the edge of a
steep street-front slope,
this limestone-lined entertainment
patio enjoys great views and—
due to its height—privacy as
well. Double sets of wide French
doors give access from the kitchen.

inside out

IN TEMPERATE CLIMATES, you can relax the line between indoors and outdoors, creating a leisurely transition between the two. The effect begins with your choice of patio doors. French and sliding models are time-honored options, but consider other types, too: folding, pivoting, pocket, and overhead. You can also group glazed doors with operable or fixed window units to make a window wall that seems to merge directly into the landscape.

To further the effect, consider using the same paving inside and out. Because tile and stone both look great indoors, they're popular flooring choices for an indoor room that's related to a patio as well as for the patio itself. Poured concrete is showing up, too, especially in modernistic design schemes.

Enclosed patios form effective bridges between indoor and outdoor living spaces. Use arbors, trellises, and screens to define a transition zone. In harsh climates, the sun-room is an option as an indoor-outdoor space. Some sun-rooms can be opened up when the sun shines and battened down when hard winds blow.

If you're planning a new home or an extensive remodel, you may wish to incorporate an interior courtyard, or atrium, into your plans, perhaps one accessed from several interior rooms. And don't rule out the classic porch, currently enjoying a deserved comeback.

With the flick of a wrist, the segmented roof above this outdoor dining room silently changes from an open trellis to partially angled louvers for sun control, then becomes a closed, watertight surface.

Two sets of multifold doors open the side and end of this living room to a jasmine-shrouded patio. To further blur the distinction between inside and outside, a fossilized flagstone floor runs throughout.

Homeowners in a temperate climate stretched their indoor living space by fashioning an outdoor living room complete with couches, spa, and a lighting scheme that's also an echo of the indoor lighting.

When the owners of this home are feeling cooped up but it's too damp or windy to go out in the yard, they retreat to the indoor-outdoor garden room off the rear bedroom of their house. The brick-floored addition is open to the air at the top of both ends and in the arched doorway, but the side walls and glazed roof panels provide protection from the weather.

The classic porch is, of course, a time-tested way to bridge house and garden. This one fronts a turn-of-the-century historical dwelling faced with massive chunks of local granite. Rustic tiles pave the elevated floor; traditional furnishings add period ambience.

great patios and decks

remote retreats

Blue chairs and a white arbor are tinged with yellow sunrise light. The owner-built structure, floored with flagstone and soft star creeper, perches atop an east-facing hillside garden and makes a great vantage point for morning or evening views.

GETTING AWAY FROM IT ALL gets tougher and tougher, but a detached patio or deck can offer restful privacy while utilizing an otherwise undeveloped garden area.

It can be tiny. A small paved clearing, borrowed from the garden, might contain just enough solid brick to anchor a bench or chairs, drinks, and a thick novel or two.

Or it can be more substantial. A freestanding deck or a bower (a rustic shelter with arbor roof, built-in bench, and perhaps a trickling fountain) might perch above a distant view or face inward to a quiet reflecting pond.

Gazebos are being rediscovered. Evocative of country bandstands on summer evenings, they become poetic-looking retreats and romantic garden destinations. The traditional gazebo has either six or eight sides and sloping rafters joined in a central hub at the roof peak. Newer, looser interpretations can be husky—with hefty corner columns and stacked beams—or quite airy, consisting of little more than four posts connected by pairs of 2 by 6s.

Remote retreats take beautifully to amenities: decorative path lights or downlights, hammocks or swings, fountains or spas. Make the route to your hideaway direct or circuitous; mark the spot with a clearly visible overhead structure or use subtle screening and tall plantings as camouflage.

A symbol of repose, this secluded teahouse sits atop a low-level platform deck that rests on sturdy boulders amidst lush plantings, waterfalls, and a pond that's home to flickering orange koi.

Some gardens just cry out for a meandering path and a
remote sitting area or two. This small clearing is sparely
floored with square concrete paver blocks; the winding
path moves onward to several other hidden spots.

This quiet clearing, seemingly returning to the elements, blends an engulfing carpet of beach grasses with just enough weathered railroad ties to support two chairs and a few container plants.

An aggregate path leads toward the wooden bridge and onward to a traditional gazebo, sited in a quiet corner away from the bustle of house and patio. Waterfall and stream add a sound track to simple daydreaming or moon-watching.

going vertical

AN ARBOR OR TRELLIS launches your landscape into another dimension—the vertical—while doubling as an accent, shelter, plant support, or privacy screen.

A trellis is typically a simple, flat framework of vertical supports and horizontal crosspieces. An arbor takes flanking trellis walls and adds a trellis-like roof; classic arch arbors curve this roof. A beefier, longer arbor, laid out in colonnade fashion, becomes a pergola, traditionally shored up with stout timber posts or cast columns.

You can make your own trellis or buy a commercial model at a garden center or through a mail-order supplier. Some types are made of sturdy dimension lumber, some of wooden strips or lattice, and others of sturdier wrought iron. Whatever the material, the trellis must be strong enough to support the weight of mature plants and durable enough to stand up to the rigors of your climate.

A classical poolside loggia is ready for a quiet summer evening's repose. Besides shade and style, overhead structures like this furnish hidden anchors for outdoor light fixtures.

A green-painted, garage-attached arbor harbors a cooling crop of shady grape leaves and shelters a gravel-lined pocket patio. It also supports an old-fashioned porch swing.

Whether freestanding or attached to a building, an arbor is held up by a series of posts or columns. These support horizontal beams, which usually support rafters. In a house-attached structure, a ledger takes the place of a beam, and the rafters are laid directly on the ledger. The rafters can be either left uncovered or covered with lath, lattice, poles, grape stakes, or solid panels.

Morning sun angles across an aggregate patio that's backed by a long, open pergola. An informal garden path flows through this tunnel which, besides dividing garden spaces and supporting a thick growth of vines, also forms a handy support for hanging plants and garden ornaments.

An evenly spaced grid of traditional painted lath forms a stylish privacy screen and, with the peaked framework overhead, helps create a rather formal outdoor room.

A lazy-making hammock is one of the great pleasures of summer, but trees sturdy enough to support one are not always handy. Here the solution is a slender arbor with two hefty 6-by-6 posts spaced 13 feet apart.

great patios and decks

the outdoor kitchen

Built of rustic brick, an outdoor kitchen houses a gas-fired barbecue and griddle, metal-doored storage cabinets, and a tiled countertop. The arbor above provides shade and some shelter, and helps define the space.

FAMILY COOKOUTS and entertaining are often centered around the barbecue. But although the familiar kettle shape may still preside over the proceedings, you can go a step further—and bring the comfort and convenience of an indoor kitchen to poolside or patio.

The layout of your outdoor kitchen and your choice of cooking elements will depend on your favorite cooking technique, whether it's grilling, stir-frying, or griddle cooking. Commercial barbecues and cooktops abound. More sophisticated masonry units incorporate built-in smokers, commercial-quality woks, or pizza ovens that accompany a traditional grill.

Facilities around the barbecue may include preparation and serving areas, storage cabinets, a vent hood, an under-counter refrigerator, a sink with disposal, a dishwasher, a wet bar, and a dining area. Built-in entertainment centers with TV or audio/intercom systems are other possible additions.

This wood-fired outdoor oven sees plenty of pizza-baking and chicken-roasting action. The carefully crafted granite structure houses a prefabricated oven insert, a chimney, a wood bin, and even a digital timer. Nearby are handy built-in stone countertops and a gas-fired barbecue.

Maintaining and cleaning outdoor cooking facilities can be a challenge. If you use protective grill covers and rugged materials such as concrete or tile, you can clean the kitchen area simply by hosing it down.

Many outdoor kitchens are at least partially sheltered overhead or housed in a gazebo. Depending on the site's exposure and microclimate, you may need to add screens, trellises, or even heavy-duty bifold or sliding doors to help screen wind and hot sun or provide temporary enclosure during winter months.

A granite-tiled eating counter (right) backs a curved entertaining area that's fully integrated into a poolside patio design. The well-equipped kitchen area (above) is set two steps below general patio level, making serving and conversing more comfortable. The lowered floor also encourages swimmers to join in, using the tile-topped "tables" along the pool's edge.

Though canopied by lush foliage, this outdoor dining area contains everything necessary for a casual meal: gas barbecue, sink, refrigerator, ice-maker, cabinets, teak dining table, and folding rattan chairs.

great patios and decks

a splash of water

IN RECENT YEARS swimming pools have been slimmed to fit home landscapes rather than overpower them. Some can be shoehorned into tight sites and integrated more easily into relatively modest schemes. The lap pool is a case in point.

If you're planning a pool, also provide a paved area or deck adjoining it. As a general rule, the poolside area should be at least equal to the area of the pool itself, and should drain away from the pool. Nonslip masonry is safest, but wood stays cooler underfoot. The surround sets the mood: with the addition of boulders, flagstones, bridges, and other free-form edgings, naturalistic pools and spas can double as garden ponds.

Spas come in a rainbow of colors, shapes, and textures; materials range from sleek acrylic to formal concrete. Wooden hot tubs, a cousin from California, resemble large, usually straight-sided barrels. Place your spa or hot tub poolside or sequester it in a private nook. Be sure to plan shelter from wind, rain, and the neighbors.

Whether trickling as a wall fountain, meandering as a stream, or collected as a full-scale garden pond complete with lilies and fish, a decorative water feature brings a sense of magic and repose to the outdoor environment. Your pond may be formal or informal, edged with angular brick, or rimmed with native boulders. And it needn't be built in; even the tiniest layout can make way for a tub garden or a small spill fountain.

The house tucks in beside the lap pool and opens to it through a sliding glass wall from the living room. The pool was there first: the rebuilt house was designed to incorporate it.

A foreground spa, two garden ponds, and a swimming pool (not shown) all nest efficiently in this backyard scene. Wood decking ties all the elements together and provides a platform for a leisurely stroll.

*Flagstone paving reflects warm evening colors in a
dramatic "vanishing-edge" pool, seemingly cantilevered
beyond the canyon rim (the secret is a retaining wall
hidden from sight, plus a recirculating pump). Boulders
form massive accents, setting off both waterfall and spa. A
poolside oak grows inside a circular well.*

The pleasing pastels of tiled borders in pool and spa are repeated in intricate mosaic murals behind both fountain and serving counter, pulling this broad poolside entertainment area together visually.

Formal as can be, the view through this classical masonry arch highlights a wall fountain, a marble-lined spa, and the enclosed courtyard patio beyond.

A detached patio surrounds a formal water garden. The concrete pavers are rigidly rectangular, but softened by abundant border plantings. The pond is home to thick-growing water lilies; spray fountains add sound and movement to the colorful spectacle.

This built-in spa, adjacent to a master bedroom, features a retractable teak cover that slides on steel tracks recessed in the concrete-and-terrazzo patio. When the cover is closed, it doubles as a small low-level deck.

Three water features in one, this combination wall fountain/spa/garden pond contrasts diagonal tile diamonds in glossy colors with an earthier backdrop of conventional brick.

great patios and decks

finishing touches

DON'T FORGET the custom touches that can turn a hardscape into a comfortable outdoor room.

Safety, security, and decor can all be improved with a good outdoor lighting scheme. The only restriction is to keep both glare and wattage at a low level. Because the contrast between darkness and a light source is so great, glare can be a problem at night. Three rules of thumb: choose shielded fixtures; place fixtures out of sight lines; and lower overall light levels. A little light goes a long way at night. You can choose a standard 120-volt system or use a low-voltage scheme. For additional details, see pages 106–107.

When it comes to seating, opt for freestanding, portable patio furniture or built-ins or both. Architectural built-ins supplement portable patio furniture and free up floor space for other uses. Build benches into wide steps or transitions between levels. Make them from nonslip masonry, wood, or metal, and plan carefully for drainage. For fun, add overhead support for a porch swing or hammock.

Portable containers can bring annuals and perennials, shrubs, and even vegetables to any favorable location. On the other hand, built-in planting spaces lend a custom look to your structure. Add formal masonry beds or leave planting pockets between paving units (run drip tubing below the surface). Incorporate planters into steps or level changes.

This front-yard fireplace helps turn a gentle slope into an entertainment area. Courtyard paving is level with the house's floor for easier indoor-outdoor passage. A heavy-beamed trellis scales down the tall chimney.

A slatted wood porch swing complements the warm tones of variegated sandstone paving.

*An entry patio's vividly colored
bench-wall conceals seated
guests from the street beyond.
The same acrylic house paint
was used for house walls and
the bench; flagstones top the
table and form footrests along
the curve of the bench's base.*

*A simple but graceful patio planter bed doubles as a
bench; the stuccoed knee wall is capped with bent wood.
The pocket cactus garden keeps patio loungers alert.*

A multilayered forest of oaks and madrones gains almost magical drama through carefully placed deck lighting that picks up tree shapes and depth. The 150-watt uplights are mounted to a deck fascia; softer downlights (to guide foot traffic), mounted to the house siding, are fitted with glare-reducing louvers.

Subtle night lighting highlights plantings and helps turn an arbor-topped patio into an around-the-clock extension of interior space. Discreet downlights provide ambient and accent light; strip lights along horizontal beams are almost purely for fun.

Plant containers offer seasonal flexibility and help blur the borders between hardscape and garden. Containers can be portable, like the stone iguana pot shown above; they can be built-in, like the (bottomless) steel culvert pipes at top right; or they can leave the ground entirely, like the hanging pot at right.

What can you do with a narrow patioside planting bed that's backed by boring stucco walls? This twiggy trellis, shaped like a four-paneled screen, has horizontal grids built from birch branches fastened to 1¹/₂-inch spacers screwed into the house wall. The arching tops are formed by bundles of whiplike birch twigs bound together with copper wire.

Morning sun casts tulip shadows across tightly fitted

flagstone paving. The elliptic shape of this planting pocket

gives it an informal, unpredictable quality.

A SHOPPER'S GUIDE

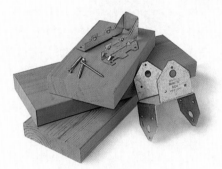

WHETHER YOUR PREFERENCE is for wood or masonry, this chapter can help you sort out your options. Here we focus on flooring materials for your new outdoor recreation space. We'll try to demystify some of the ritual and jargon surrounding lumberyards and garden centers. Special features along the way help you understand the intricacies of lumber specifications, concrete make-overs, and outdoor heating and lighting. **LOCAL INFORMATION** can be a big help. Ask your building department or garden supplier about the best deck stain, tile type, or base treatment for use in your area. Be sure to survey current local offerings before buying; new products appear constantly. **IF YOU'RE BUILDING** the project yourself, you may wish to consult the Sunset titles *The Complete Deck Book* and *The Complete Patio Book* for detailed help.

Lumberyard Primer

A CRASH COURSE IN DECKING LINGO

Because wood comes in so many sizes, species, and grades, a visit to a lumberyard can be a daunting experience for the uninitiated. Busy salespeople may not be adequately responsive if you're completely unfamiliar with deck-building terminology. But once you know a few basics, it's easier to get help with the fine points.

Basic deck components are shown on page 23.

Lumber terms

Your choice in lumber, which will take the biggest bite out of your project budget, strongly influences the appearance of your deck. It pays to explore the options carefully before you make a final plan.

SOFTWOOD OR HARDWOOD? All woods are one or the other. The terms don't refer to a wood's relative hardness, but to the kind of tree from which it comes. Softwoods come from evergreens (conifers), hardwoods from broad-leafed (deciduous) trees.

Decks are generally built from softwoods. However, more economical offerings of hardwoods such as mahogany, angico, and plantation-grown teak (the boat builder's favorite) have recently entered the market.

HEARTWOOD AND SAPWOOD. A wood's properties are determined by the part of the tree from which it came. The inactive wood nearest the center of a living tree is called heartwood. Sapwood, next to the bark, contains the growth cells. Heartwood is more resistant to decay; sapwood is more porous and absorbs preservatives and other chemicals more efficiently.

Among heartwoods, the most decay-resistant and termite-proof species you can buy are redwood and cedar. This durability, combined with their natural beauty, makes them favorites for decking. On the other

hand, they are softer, weaker, and more expensive than ordinary structural woods such as Douglas fir and Southern pine. To get the best of both worlds, most professional designers use fir or another structural wood for a deck's substructure, but redwood or cedar for decking, benches, and railings. For any wood nearer than 6 inches to the ground or to concrete foundations, though, choose decay-resistant heartwood or pressure-treated wood (see facing page).

GRADES. Lumber is sorted and graded at the mill. Generally, lumber grades represent several factors: natural growth characteristics (such as knots); defects resulting from milling errors; and commercial drying and preserving treatments that affect strength, durability, and appearance.

The higher the grade, the better

ALASKAN YELLOW CEDAR

CLEAR HEART REDWOOD

CONSTRUCTION HEART REDWOOD

the wood—and the more you will have to pay. One way to save money on your project is to choose the most appropriate grade (not necessarily the highest grade) for each element.

Redwood is usually graded for its appearance and for the percentage of heartwood versus sapwood it contains. Among pure heartwoods, Clear All Heart is the best grade, then B Heart, Construction Heart, and Merchantable Heart, in descending order.

Cedar grades, starting with the highest quality, are Architect Clear, Architect Knotty, and Custom Knotty. These grades don't indicate whether the lumber is heartwood or sapwood.

ROUGH AND SURFACED LUMBER. Most lumberyards handle both rough and surfaced lumber. Rough lumber tends to be available only in lower grades, with a correspondingly greater number of defects and a higher moisture content. Surfaced lumber, the standard for most construction and a must for formal decking, comes in nearly all grades.

NOMINAL AND SURFACED SIZES. Be aware that a finished "2 by 4" is not 2 inches thick by 4 inches wide. The nominal size of lumber is designated before the piece is dried and surfaced, so the finished size is smaller. Here are some examples:

2 by 3 = 1½" by 2½"
2 by 4 = 1½" by 3½"
2 by 6 = 1½" by 5½"
4 by 4 = 3½" by 3½"

You may also run across decking boards with thickness designated in fractions—for example, "⁵⁄₄." This traditional hardwood term means "five-quarter" or a nominal 1¼ inches (⁴⁄₄ would indicate a 1-inch thickness). The actual thickness of these surfaced boards is usually about ¼ inch less than the nominal measurement.

Treated lumber

Though redwood and cedar heartwoods resist decay and termites, other woods that contact the ground or trap water may quickly rot and lose their strength. For this reason, less durable types such as Southern pine and Western hem/fir are often factory-treated with preservatives to protect them from rot, insects, and other sources of decay. These woods are generally less expensive and in many areas more readily available than redwood or cedar. They can be used for surface decking as well as for structural members such as posts, beams, and joists.

Working with treated lumber isn't always a pleasure. Compared with redwood and cedar, which are easy to cut and nail or screw, treated wood is often hard and brittle and more likely to warp or twist. Moreover, some people object to its typically greenish brown color (applying a stain can conceal it) and the staplelike incisions that usually cover it (some types come without these marks).

Because the primary preservative used contains chromium, a toxic metal, you should wear safety glasses and a dust mask when cutting treated lumber, and you should never burn it.

HOGANY

ANGICO

PRESSURE-TREATED HEM/FIR

DECK SCREWS

Deck hardware

Nails, screws, and deck clips secure your decking to the framing below. The fasteners you choose help create the strength of your finished deck and also affect its appearance.

NAILS. Box or common nails are used for most outdoor deck construction. Buy hot-dipped galvanized, aluminum, or stainless steel nails; other types will rust. In fact, even

GALVANIZED BOX NAILS

the best hot-dipped nail will rust in time, particularly at the exposed head, where its coating has been battered by a hammer.

A nail's length is indicated by a "penny" designation ("penny" is abbreviated as "d," from the Latin *denarius*). Most decking jobs are done with 8d (2½") and 16d (3½") nails.

DECK SCREWS. Though more expensive than nails, coated or galvanized deck screws provide several advantages: they don't pop up as readily, their coating is less likely to be damaged during installation, and their use eliminates the possibility of hammer dents in the decking.

Choose screws that are long enough to penetrate joists at least as deep as

---

NEW LUMBER ALTERNATIVES

Shrinking forests and dwindling supplies of quality lumber have encouraged the timely development of both environmentally sensitive wood products and engineered materials suitable for decks and other garden structures.

When it comes to lumber, you might consider woods other than the best grades of redwood and cedar, which generally come from the oldest trees. Instead, seek out plantation-grown woods or those from certified forests; or look for suppliers of salvaged lumber from orchards or demolished buildings.

Some manufacturers are also combining landfill-bound wood with waste plastic to produce so-called "wood-polymer composites." Though

not meant for structural purposes, these weatherproof products can be used for decking and railings. Available in several colors, they can also be painted or stained and cut,

drilled, and shaped like standard lumber. For families with young children, these synthetic boards have the additional advantage of being splinter-free.

Made from recycled wood and plastics, new synthetic decking "boards" can stand in for traditional lumber.

DECK CLIPS

the decking is thick (for 2 by 4 or 2 by 6 decking, buy 2½- or 3-inch screws).

DECK CLIPS. To keep fasteners from showing, you can use special deck-fastening clips. Nailed to the sides of decking lumber and secured to joists, these fasteners hide between deck boards. Deck clips also elevate boards off the joists a hair, discouraging the rot that wood-to-wood contact may foster. On the down side, clips are more expensive to buy and install than nails or screws.

Deck finishes

There's no substitute for using decay-resistant wood like heart redwood or pressure-treated lumber in places where deck members come in contact with soil or are embedded in concrete. Applying a water repellent, a semitransparent stain, or a solid-color stain can, however, protect other parts of a deck and preserve the wood's beauty.

Whatever product you choose, it's best to try it on a sample board before committing your entire deck to it. Always read labels: some products should not be applied over new wood; others may require the application of a sealer first.

WATER REPELLENTS. Also known as water sealers, these products protect decking wood. Clear sealers won't color wood, but they darken it slightly. These products allow the wood to gradually fade to a neutral gray. You can buy them in either oil- or water-base versions. Many formulations include both UV-blockers and mildewcides. Some brands come in slightly tinted, dye-color versions.

Don't use clear surface finishes such as spar varnish or polyurethane on decks. They wear quickly and are very hard to renew. They're also expensive.

SEMITRANSPARENT STAINS. These contain enough pigment to tint the wood's surface but not enough to mask the natural grain completely. You can find both water- and oil-base versions. Usually one coat is sufficient. Besides stains in traditional gray and wood tones, you'll find products for "reviving" a deck's color or for dressing up pressure-treated wood.

SOLID-COLOR STAINS. These are essentially paints; their heavy pigments cover the wood's grain completely. You can usually get any available paint color mixed into a solid deck-stain base. But even though these products are formulated to withstand foot traffic, you'll probably have to renew them frequently.

Deck finishes offer plentiful choices in color and protection. Shown at right, from top to bottom: unfinished redwood board; clear water sealer; tinted oil-base repellent; semitransparent gray stain; and red solid-color stain.

Brick

SET IN SAND OR IN MORTAR—EITHER WAY, IT'S A CLASSIC

Brick's use dates back at least 6,000 years. To make bricks, clay is mixed with water, then hand-molded or machine-extruded into traditional forms, then fired in a kiln. A rich palette of colors and a broad range of styles make brick a perennial favorite for garden paving.

Countless patterns can be created when designing with brick, and each one elicits a slightly different response. Six of the most popular are shown on the facing page.

Brick types

Of the bewildering variety of bricks available, only two basic kinds are

Brick samples range from machine-extruded common type (far left) to brand-new "used" bricks to hand-molded ones (far right). Color comes from the chemical composition of the clay and the firing method and temperature.

used for garden construction: rough-textured common brick and smoother-surfaced face brick.

Most garden paving is done with common brick. People like its familiar, warm color and texture, and it's less expensive than face brick. Common brick is more porous than face brick and less uniform in size and color (common bricks may vary up to ¼ inch in length).

Face brick, with its sand-finished, glazed surface, is not as widely available as common brick. More often used for facing buildings than for paving, this brick is best reserved for elegant raised beds, attractive edgings, and other accents where its smoothness won't present a safety hazard.

In addition to the familiar orange-red, some manufacturers offer bricks in colors created by the addition of chemicals to the clay. Manganese can give a metallic blue tone. Iron pro-

duces a dark speckling. "Flashed" brick is fired unevenly to darken either its face (large surface) or edge.

Used brick has uneven surfaces and streaks of old mortar that can look very attractive in an informal pavement. Manufactured "used" or "rustic" bricks cost about the same as the genuine article and are easier to find. Fire-bricks, blond-colored and porous, provide interesting accents but don't wear well as general paving.

The typical brick is about 8 by 4 by 2⅜ inches thick. "Paver" bricks, which are made to use atop a concrete base, are roughly half the thickness of standard bricks. "True" (or "mortar-less") pavers are a uniform 4 by 8 inches (plus or minus ⅛ inch) and can be invaluable for laying a complex pattern with tightly butted joints. To calculate the exact amount of brick you'll need for a project, visit a building supplier first, measuring tape in hand.

All outdoor bricks are graded according to their ability to withstand weathering. If you live in a region where it regularly freezes and thaws, buy only bricks graded SW, which indicates they can withstand changing weather conditions.

Sand or mortar?

Brick set in sand or rock fines (a mix of grain sizes) is casual-looking and less uniform than mortared brick, with more textural variation (for a construction detail, see page 21). This method allows percolation, which is important when installing a patio over tree roots. Bricks in sand can move around and may eventually have to be reset, but repairs are easier than with grouted bricks.

When set in mortar and grouted, brick has cleaner lines, which can give a design a more formal or contemporary look. The surface is easier to maintain and safer for walking in high heels, as long as joints are wider than ¼ inch. The grout becomes an important part of the design. Browns soften or blend with the pattern, whereas lighter colors, providing contrast, may emphasize it.

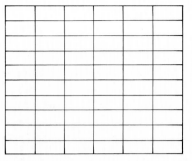

JACK ON JACK

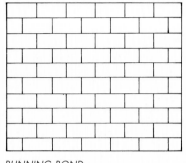

RUNNING BOND

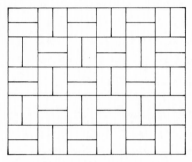

BASKET WEAVE

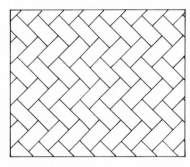

HERRINGBONE

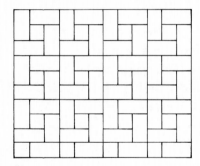

PINWHEEL

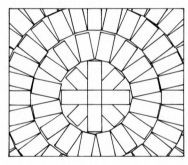

WHORLED

Concrete

FLUID NEW SHAPES, EARTHY COLORS, AND SOFT TEXTURES

Though often unfairly dismissed as cold and forbidding, poured—or more accurately, cast—concrete is even more adaptable than brick. Used with the proper forms and reinforcement (see page 21), concrete can conform to almost any shape. It can be lightly smoothed or heavily brushed, surfaced with colorful pebbles, swirled, scored, tinted or painted, patterned, or molded to resemble another material. And if you get tired of the concrete surface later on, you can use it as a foundation for a new pavement of brick, stone, or tile set in mortar.

Shopping for concrete

Strictly speaking, concrete is a mixture of portland cement, sand, aggregate, and water. Cement is what binds everything together and gives the fin-

ished product its hardness. The sand and aggregate (usually gravel) act as fillers and control shrinkage.

Buying bagged, dry, ready-mixed concrete is expensive but convenient, especially for small jobs. The standard 90-pound bag makes ⅔ cubic foot of concrete, enough to cover about a 16-inch-square area 4 inches deep.

If your project is fairly large, it pays to order portland cement, sand, and aggregate in bulk and mix them by hand or with a power mixer. Some dealers also supply trailers containing about 1 cubic yard of wet, ready-mixed concrete (about enough for an 8- by 10-foot patio). For larger-scale work, a commercial transit-mix truck can deliver enough concrete to fill large patio forms in a single pour.

Exact formulas of concrete vary from area to area, depending on local

climate, season, and materials. In areas with severe freeze-thaw cycles, you'll need to add an air-entraining agent to prevent cracking. Be sure to ask your supplier about the best formula for your needs. If you're using ready-mixed, figure about .37 cubic yards of concrete for every 10 cubic feet.

Jazzing it up

Concrete pavings are typically given some type of surface treatment, both for appearance's sake and to provide traction.

You can wash or sandblast concrete to uncover the aggregate. Or embed colorful pebbles and stones in it (this finish, generally known as seeded aggregate, is probably the most popular contemporary paving surface). The addition of larger river rocks and field-stones can also give new interest to a dull slab.

Other ways to modify standard steel-troweled concrete surfaces include color-dusting, staining, masking, sandblasting, acid-washing, and salt-finishing. A professional can also stamp and tint concrete to resemble stone, tile, or brick. Stamped patterns simulate either butted joints or open ones, which can then be grouted to look like unit masonry.

A basic concrete recipe includes portland cement, sand, aggregate, and water.

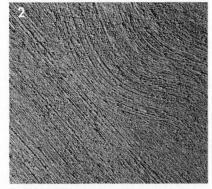

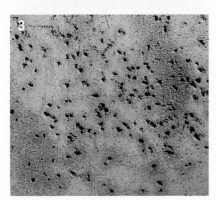

Creating a softer look

Several techniques can allow concrete to be used pleasingly in a more casual environment. You can also leave planting pockets in a freshly poured slab, then fill them with soil and plants.

Or dig holes or shape curved forms and fill them with concrete. The resulting pads—with planting spaces in between—can be smoothed, textured, or seeded with aggregate.

Shown above are six basic concrete finishes. Semismooth texture (1) is achieved with a wooden float. Broomed surface (2) is best where maximum traction is needed. Rock salt (3), exposed aggregate (4), and travertine (5) are three popular decorative finishes. Stone-tile pattern (6) is one of many stamping possibilities.

CONCRETE MAKE-OVERS

If you have a deteriorating concrete patio or driveway, you can either demolish it and build anew or, in some cases, give it a face-lift. Asphalt is usually best removed, but an existing concrete slab, unless heavily damaged, can serve admirably as a base for brick, pavers, tile, or stone. Another possibility is to construct a low-level deck over the slab.

Professionally applied solutions include the treatment of concrete with one of three methods: bonding, staining, or topcoating.

In bonding, a mixture of colored cement and a binder is sprayed over the entire surface. Then a design is created by the use of incised patterns or imitation grout lines.

Several companies offer chemical stains in a variety of colors that can be applied directly to the surface of an existing slab to give it a camouflaging patina.

One innovative top coat is made of ground-up bits of colored recycled rubber bonded together with a clear epoxy. Or you can cover the concrete with seeded aggregate. Or float on a new colored mix, which can then be stamped or textured.

Concrete Pavers

NEWLY STYLISH, BUT STILL TOUGH ENOUGH FOR TRAFFIC

Available in many sizes, colors, and textures, concrete pavers are no longer limited to the ubiquitous 12-inch squares you've seen for years. Paver shapes now include circles, rectangles, triangles, and contours that interlock. Easily installed atop a packed sand bed (see page 21), pavers are an ideal choice for do-it-yourselfers.

Paver possibilities

A simple square can be part of a grid or even a gentle arc. Squares or rectangles can butt together to create broad unbroken surfaces, or they can be spaced apart and surrounded with grass, a ground cover, or gravel for textural interest.

Interlocking pavers fit together like jigsaw puzzle pieces. Made of extremely dense concrete that is pressure-formed in special machines and laid in sand with closed (butted) joints, they form a surface more rigid than brick. No paver can tip out of alignment without taking several of its neighbors with it; thus, the surface remains intact even under very substantial loads. Interlocking pavers are available in tan, brown, red, and natural gray, plus blends of these colors.

Modern cobblestone blocks are very popular for casual gardens. Butt them tightly together and then sweep sand or soil between the irregular edges.

Turf blocks, a special paver variant, are designed to carry light traffic while retaining and protecting ground-cover plants. These suggest the possibility of grassy patios and driveways, and can create side-yard access routes that stand up to wear.

Concrete "bricks," available in classic red as well as imitation used or antique styles, are increasingly popular as substitutes for the real thing, and in many areas cost significantly less.

Shopping for pavers

Circles, squares, and rectangles can be found at most building and garden supply centers. Some interlocking shapes are proprietary, available only at a few outlets or directly from distributors. To locate these, check the yellow pages under "Concrete Products."

Some professionals cast their own pavers in custom shapes, textures, and colors—mimicking adobe, stone, or tile, for example.

Be cautious when choosing colored concrete pavers. The pigment in some is very shallow, and bare concrete may show through deep scratches or chips.

HEATING IT UP

You may want to consider adding some type of heating device to your new patio or deck to take the edge off the weather and increase the hours and days you can spend outdoors.

A fireplace is one way to go. But using a patio heater is a quicker way to turn your outdoor room into a pleasant place to spend a brisk evening. You can buy a freestanding heater or install a more permanent gas or electric unit, which may prove more effective and less visible.

A stainless steel mushroom heater (right), also known as an umbrella, radiates its warming rays from the top cylinder. A gas-fired directional heater (left) mounts to a house's eaves, allowing it to throw heat efficiently without being obtrusive.

For a heating unit to perform well, you must place it in the right location. Shelter it from the wind. Pick a spot to heat that's intimate and comfortable. For extra warmth, place your heater near a wall or other solid structure so the heat can radiate back into your seating area.

Be sure to block any breeze at ground level so your feet won't get cold while you're sitting outside.

Standard paver offerings (facing page) include "stepping-stones," turf blocks, and various brick and cobblestone look-alikes. Interlocking pavers (left) fit together like puzzle pieces. Custom-made units (above) are subtler, resembling stone and ceramic tile.

Ceramic Tile

TILE TURNS BLAND LANDSCAPES INTO LIVELY OUTDOOR ROOMS

Tile works well in both formal and informal garden situations. Its typically earthy tones blend with natural colors outdoors, and the hand-fired pigments are permanent and nonfading. Because tile looks great indoors, too, it's a good flooring choice for an indoor room that relates to a patio as well as for the patio itself.

Heavy tiles that are at least ¾ inch thick can be laid in a sand bed. However, the most stable bed for any tile is a 1-inch mortar bed over an existing concrete slab or a newly poured one (for details, see page 21).

Glazed or unglazed?

Glaze is a hard finish, usually colored, applied to the clay surface before final baking. Most bright, flashy tiles you see in tile displays are glazed.

Unless a special grit is added to glazed tiles, they can make treacherous footing when wet. For paving, it's best to use unglazed tiles, reserving their shiny counterparts for occasional accents or for edgings or raised planting beds.

Outdoor types

In cold climates, your tile choice must be freeze-thaw stable. So-called impervious and vitreous tiles, including quarry tiles and unglazed porcelain, are the best choices here. In milder climates, terra-cotta can hold its own.

PORCELAIN PAVERS

Porcelain pavers can be made to resemble slate, limestone, and other stones, but come in straightforward pastel colors, too. While many tiles are polished, more slip-resistant textures include split (resembling slate) and sandblasted surfaces and surfaces embossed with raised grids. Though 12-inch square pavers are standard, sizes range from 4- by 6-inch rectangles up through 24-inch squares.

Tough quarry tiles are made by the extrusion process (picture a giant pasta machine)—you can usually identify them by roller grooves on their backs. Though some quarry tiles are glazed, most come unglazed in natural clay

colors of yellow, brown, rust, or red. Some exhibit "flashing," heat-produced shadings that vary from tile to tile. Typical sizes are 6 by 6, 8 by 8, and 12 by 12 inches. You'll also find some rectangles and a smattering of hexagons.

Translated from the Italian, terra-cotta means "cooked earth." But whether you see terra-cotta in antique French folk tiles, hand-formed Mexican slabs (known as Saltillo tiles), or rustic Italian or Portuguese wares, the charm of this material lies in its very lack of consistency. Terra-cotta tiles come as squares, rectangles, hexagons, and octagons, as well as in Moorish, ogee, and other interlocking shapes. These tiles are generally nonvitreous and highly absorbent, and so are questionable for outdoor use in cold climates.

To seal or not to seal?

Some unglazed tiles are sealed at the factory. Unsealed, unglazed units such as terra-cotta and some quarry tiles need to be sealed for protection against surface water and stains.

Surface or top sealers offer the most resistance to stains but darken tiles and produce a sheen that you may or may not find appealing. These coatings must also be stripped and reapplied periodically.

Penetrating sealers soak into the tile instead of sitting on its surface. But they're not as protective as top sealers.

Sealer technology is changing all the time, and some proprietary formulas vary from region to region. Explain your intended use to a knowledgeable local dealer and ask for a specific recommendation. Be sure to inquire about maintenance requirements.

Whatever sealer you select, it's best to test its appearance on a sample tile before you apply it to your entire patio.

QUARRY TILES

TERRA-COTTA TILES

Stone

GO NATIVE—IN FORMAL OR INFORMAL STYLE

Stone pavings have the appeal of a thoroughly natural material, and most are very durable. Flat flagstones and cut stone tiles are both ideal for formal patios. For a more informal look, try setting irregularly shaped rocks and pebbles in mortar or directly in the soil.

Flagstone

Technically, flagstone is any flat stone that's either naturally thin or split from rock that cleaves easily. The selection pictured below gives you an idea of the range of colors and textures available at masonry and building supply yards. Costs depend on where you live in relation to where the stone originates: the farther from the quarry, the higher the price. Expect to find natural color variations within each type of stone.

When selecting flagstone for outdoor paving, think of how it will be used. Formal entry and entertaining areas should be smooth surfaces, safely accommodating high heels. Patios that serve as sitting and dining areas also need a level surface for chairs and tables; select a stone with a fairly smooth surface. Also, some types of flagstones (notably sandstones) are porous and may be difficult to maintain under dining areas or near messy fruit trees. Some kinds can be slippery when wet.

Flagstones come in various thicknesses. The thinnest (also called

veneer) range from ¼ to ¾ inch thick, and should be laid on a stout, 4-inch-thick concrete slab. Thicker stones are typically laid in mortar atop a thinner concrete base (see page 21). Or, for a more casual look, consider setting stones in sand and adding plants between the joints.

Stone tiles

Many stone types are available precut in rectangular shapes. Popular tiles include those made from slate, sandstone, granite, quartzite, limestone, travertine (a pitted limestone that may be "filled"), and adoquin (a dense volcanic stone).

Outdoor tiles must be slip resistant. Naturally textured stones, including split slates and sandstones, are traditional choices. Other attractive slip-resistant textures are achieved by tumbling, sandblasting, flaming, or resplitting stone tiles.

Like porous ceramic tiles, those made from soft stones, such as limestone, may need to be sealed to protect against staining and acid damage. Since sealant products are constantly changing, the best approach is to discuss your specific needs with a knowledgeable stone supplier.

Stone tiles are usually laid in mortar with very thin grout lines, which gives them a stylish, formal look. However, beefier tiles—those about 1 inch thick and thicker—can be set in sand.

Other stones

Fieldstones, river rocks, and pebbles are less expensive than flagstone and

You'll find a good selection of random-size flagstones at most masonry yards. We show some most often used, but offerings vary by region—and by supplier.

A sampler of stone tiles includes (clockwise from top): bluestone slate, flamed limestone, tumbled travertine, sandblasted quartzite, and Arizona sandstone.

LIGHTING UP THE NIGHT

Safety, security, and decoration—all three are functions of outdoor lighting, and all can be achieved with a good lighting scheme. The only restriction is the need to keep both glare and wattage at a low level.

Low-voltage or standard current?

When it's time to light up your landscape, you can choose either a standard 120-volt system or a low-voltage scheme.

Because low-voltage lights are safer, more energy efficient, and easier to install than 120-volt systems, they have become increasingly popular outdoors. Such systems use a transformer to step down household current to 12 volts. Although low-voltage fixtures lack the "punch" of line-current fixtures, their output is sufficient for many outdoor applications.

The standard 120-volt system still has some advantages outdoors. The buried cable and metallic fixtures give the installation a look of permanence; light can be projected a greater distance; and 120-volt outlets accept power tools and patio heaters.

Fixtures and bulbs

Outdoor fixtures range from well lights and other portable uplights to spread lights that illuminate paths or bridges to downlights designed to be anchored to the house wall, eaves, or trees.

Most outdoor fixtures are made of

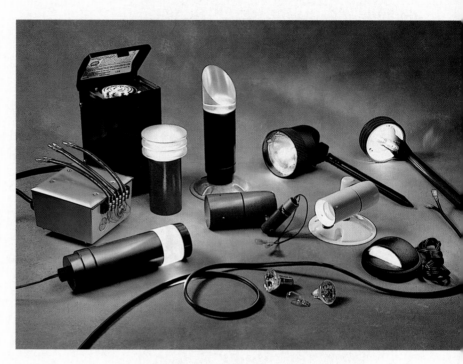

Low-voltage systems consist of transformer, timer, and easy connections to small cables run on or just below the surface. Compact, innovative fixtures include uplights, downlights, and step lights in many styles.

bronze, cast or extruded aluminum, copper, or plastic. But you can also find decorative stone, concrete, porcelain, and wood fixtures (redwood, cedar, and teak weather best). Sizes vary. When evaluating fixtures, look for gaskets, high-quality components at joints and pivot points, and locking devices for aiming the fixtures.

Choose the bulb you want first and then the appropriate fixtures. Low-voltage halogen MR-16 bulbs are popular for accenting; PAR spotlights, available in both low and standard voltage, are best to light trees or wide areas.

Less is best

Because the contrast between darkness and a light source is so great, glare can be a big problem at night. Three rules of thumb are: choose shielded fixtures; place fixtures out of sight lines; and lower overall light levels.

With a shielded light fixture, the bulb area is protected by an opaque covering that directs light away from the viewer's eyes. Instead of a hot spot of light, the eye sees the warm glow of the lighted object.

Place fixtures either very low (as along a walk) or very high. By doing

COBBLESTONE

that, you can direct them in such a way that only a play of light in the tree branches is noticed—rather than a bright glare. Use several softer lights strategically placed around the patio and yard rather than one harsh bulb.

A little light goes a long way at night. Twenty watts is strong, and even 12 watts can be very bright. If you're using line current, choose bulbs with a maximum of 50 watts.

On patios, low light levels are usually enough for conversation or dining areas. Add stronger lights for serving or barbecuing areas. Downlights are popular, but indirect lighting, diffused through plastic or another translucent material, is also useful.

Illuminating foliage can be an effective way to combine functional and decorative lighting. Decorative mini-lights help outline trees and lend sparkle to your landscape.

Strings of mini-lights are also useful for lighting steps, railings, and walkways. If your house has deep eaves or an overhang, consider placing weatherproof downlights there to conceal the fixtures while illuminating use areas.

Don't forget the view from inside. To avoid a black hole effect, try to balance light levels on both sides of a window or French doors. Use soft light in the foreground, build up the middle ground, and save the highest wattage for the background.

120-volt lighting packs a bigger punch but requires beefier components and extra safety measures. Boxes and fixtures must be sealed from weather, and wires run via buried cable or in metal conduit.

RIVER ROCKS

tile. These water-worn or glacier-ground stones form rustic pavings that make up in charm for what they lack in smoothness underfoot.

Smaller stones and pebbles can be either set in mortar or seeded into concrete. Large stones may be laid directly on the soil as raised stepping-stones. An entire surface can be paved solid with cobblestones set in concrete or tamped earth. Or use mosaic panels to break up an expanse of concrete, brick, or larger flagstones.

Some natural stones can become dangerously slick in wet weather. Because their shapes are irregular, they may be uncomfortable to walk on. It's best to confine such surfacing to a limited area.

Loose Materials

WOOD CHIPS

QUARTZ PEBBLES

RIVER ROCKS

For economy, good drainage, and a more casual look, consider including materials such as pea gravel, wood chips, or even cocoa hulls in your patio plan.

You needn't opt for the large, boring expanses that give some aggregates a bad name. Gravel can be raked into patterns or employed as a decorative element with other paving materials. You might use dividers to set off different colors and textures. Buy loose materials by the bag (small jobs only), by the ton (gravel and other rocks), or by the cubic yard.

Rock

Gravel is collected or mined from natural deposits. Crushed rock is mechanically fractured and then graded to a uniform size. If the surface of the rock has been naturally worn smooth by water, it's called river rock. Frequently, gravels are named after the regions where they were quarried.

When making a choice, consider color, sheen, texture, and size. Take home samples as you would paint chips. Keep in mind that gravel color, like paint color, looks more intense when spread over a large area.

Crushed rock compacts firmly to give stable footing on paths and walkways, but its sharp edges may hurt bare feet. Smooth river rock feels better, but tends to roll underfoot. Small river rock, also called pea gravel, is easiest to rake.

What about a glassier look? Paths or spaces between pavers may be filled with sparkling glass cullet, a gravel-like material that resembles fine beach pebbles. The glass, collected from recycled bottles, is crushed mechanically, then tumbled to smooth any sharp edges. The cullet comes in assorted colors—greens, deep amber, and clear.

Bark and by-products

Leftovers from lumber mills, wood chips and bark are springy and soft underfoot, generally inexpensive, and easy to apply. You'll probably find a wide variety of colors and textures. To work successfully as patio surfaces (rather than as mulch, for which they are also sold), they must be confined inside headers.

Shredded bark, sometimes called gorilla hair, compacts well and is especially useful as a transitional covering between patio and plantings.

Other specialized commercial by-products appear in garden centers and nurseries according to regional availability. Fresh cocoa hulls, a current favorite among West Coast landscapers, smell so pungent that chocolate fiends may want to go back to brick or concrete just to get some peace.

GORILLA HAIR

DECOMPOSED GRANITE

LAVA ROCK

COCOA HULLS

design credits

FRONT MATTER

1. Landscape designer: Roger's Gardens. 2. Landscape designer: Scott Cohen/The Green Scene. 4. Landscape architect: Mary Gordon. 5. Architect: Bokal & Sneed Architects.

A PLANNING PRIMER

6. Landscape architect: Williamson Landscape Architects. 14. Landscape architect: Jeff Stone Associates of La Jolla. 15 (top) Landscape designer: Schlegel Landscapes of Carmel. 15 (bottom) Architect and Landscape Architect: M.W. Steele Group Inc.

16. Landscape architect: Ransohoff, Blanchfield, Jones, Inc. 25. Architect: Lane Williams Architects. Landscape architect: GAYNOR Landscape Architects/Designers Inc.

GREAT PATIOS AND DECKS

26. Design: M.W. Steele Group. Contractor: Tekton Master Builders. Landscape: MartinPoirier/Spurlock Poirier Landscape Architects.

Patio Profiles

28. Landscape designer: Roger's Gardens. 29. Architect: Curtis Gelotte Architects. 30. Landscape architect: Mary Gordon.

31 (top). Landscape architect: Ransohoff, Blanchfield, Jones, Inc. Arbor design: Holger Menendez/In the Name of Design. 31 (bottom). Landscape architect: Lankford Associates. 32. Landscape architect: Delaney & Cochran. 33 (top). Mark Bartos of Hortus Garden/Design. 33 (bottom). Landscape architect: Jack Chandler & Associates. 34 (top). Design: John Copeland. 34 (bottom right). Design: Benedikt Strebel Ceramics. 35. Achitect: Brion S. Jeannette & Associates, Inc. 36. Mark Bartos of Hortus Garden/Design. 37 (bottom). Landscape architect: Delaney & Cochran. 38. Landscape designer: Schlegel Landscapes of Carmel. 39 (top). Landsacpe architect: Delaney & Cochran. 39 (bottom). Landscape architect: Robert La Rocca & Associates.

Decked Out

40. Architect: Olson Sundberg Architects. 41. Landscape architect: Williamson Landscape Architects. Architect: Snyder Hartung + Kane. Construction: John Brown Builder. 42. Landscape architect: Nick Williams & Associates. 43. Landscape architect: Lankford Associates. 44. Architect: Churchill & Hambelton Architects. 45 (top). Design: Carl & Tiffany Ledbetter, Jon Courter/Courter Construction. 45 (bottom). Landscape architect: James Bradanini, Bradanini & Associates. 46 (top). Designer: Van-Martin Rowe Design of Pasadena. 46 (bottom). Design and construction: Scott Padgett. 47. Architect: Robert Engman. 48 (top left). Design: Sean Hopper. 48 (top right). Design: Carol and Jim Stewart. 48 (bottom). Architect: Mark Meryash. 49. Design: Mike Lervick and Vicki Mandin. Contractor: Davis Construction Services.

Coping With Slopes

50. Landscape architect: Robert W. Chittock & Associates. 51. Landscape architect: R.M. Bradshaw & Associates. 52. Design: Landgraphics, Inc. 53 (both). Landscape architect: Lankford Associates.

Small Miracles

54. Landscape architect: Nick Williams & Associates. 55. Design: Artistic Botanical Creations. 56. Architect: Marquez Architecture. Tile: Ann Sachs Tile & Stone. 57 (top). Architectural designer: Kathleen McCormick. Landscape architect: Andrew Spurlock. 57 (bottom). Landscape architect: Ransohoff, Blanchfield, Jones, Inc.

Up-front Ideas

58. Designer: Van-Martin Rowe Design of Pasadena. 59. Landscape architect: The Berger Partnership. 60 (top) and 61. Design: Adams Design Associates. 60 (bottom). Designer: Van-Martin Rowe Design of Pasadena.

Inside Out

62 (bottom). Design: Eclipse Opening Roof. 63. Design: Backen, Arragoni & Ross. 64 (top). Architect: Steven Erlich Architects. 64 (bottom). Design: MGM Construction. 65. Landscape architect: The Berger Partnership.

Remote Retreats

66. Landscape architect: Lankford Associates. 67. Designer: Van-Martin Rowe Design of Pasadena. 68. Landscape architect: The Berger Partnership. 69 (bottom). Landscape architect: Ransohoff, Blanchfield, Jones, Inc.

Going Vertical

70. Landscape architect: Robert W. Chittock & Associates. 71. Designer: Van-Martin Rowe Design of Pasadena. 72. Landscape designer: Schlegel Landscapes of Carmel. 73 (top). Design: Susan

Schieson Design. 73 (bottom). Landscape architect: Jeffrey B. Glander & Associates.

The Outdoor Kitchen

74. Landscape architect: Ransohoff, Blanchfield, Jones, Inc. 75. Landscape architect: The Berger Partnership. Pizza oven: Authentic Stone & Brickwork. 76 (top) and 77. Hardscape: Southwinds Landscaping & Pools. Softscape: Roger's Gardens. 76 (bottom). Design: David Squires.

A Splash of Water

78. Architect: Steven Ehrlich Architects. 79. Landscape architect: Michael Kobayashi/ MHK Group. Additional design: American Landscape, Inc. 80. Architect: Churchill & Hambelton Architects. 81 (top). Tile artisan: Tina Ayers/Graphics in Tile. Landscape designer: Proscape Landscape Design. Interior designer: Thomas Bartlett Interiors. 81 (bottom). Landscape designer: Roger's Gardens. 82. Designers: Roger Fiske and Margo Partridge 83 (top). Architect: Olson Sundberg Architects. 83 (bottom). Landscape architect: Jeff Stone Associates of La Jolla.

Finishing Touches

84. Landscape designer: Schlegel Landscapes of Carmel. 85. Design: Steve Adams/Adams Design Associates. 86 (bottom). Architect: Morimoto Architects. 87 (top). Lighting designer: Randall Whitehead/Light Source. 87 (bottom). Architect: Backen, Arragoni & Ross. 88 (top left). Design: Jean Manocchio/Belli Fiori. 88 (top right). Landscape architect: Richard William Wogisch. 88 (center right). Design: Bud Stuckey. 88 (bottom left). Design: Kent Gordon England. Construction: Whitehill Landscape. 89. Landscape architect: Mary Gordon.

A SHOPPER'S GUIDE

90. Landscape architect: The Berger Partnership. 95 (top center). Deck clips: Deckmaster. 99 (bottom right). Landscape architect: Neil Buchanan/Glen Hurst & Associates. 101 (bottom right). Buddy Rhodes Studio. 102 and 103 (top). Galleria Tile. 103 (bottom). Fireclay Tile. 105 (top). ASN Natural Stone of San Francisco. 106 and 107 (bottom left). City Lights, Illumination Sales Corporation.

DESIGN CREDITS

110. Design: Artistic Botanical Creations. 111. Landscape designer: Scott Cohen/The Green Scene.

PHOTOGRAPHERS

Unless noted, all photographs are by Philip Harvey.

Scott Atkinson: 4, 15 (top), 30, 38, 72, 84, 89, 94 (bottom), 95 (right). Peter Christiansen: 104–105 (bottom). Glenn Cormier: 46 (bottom). Art Gray: 76 (bottom). Ken Gutmaker: 62 (bottom). Lynne Harrison: 73 (top). David Hewitt/Anne Garrison: 26, 60 (top), 61. James Frederick Housel: 49. Mark Luthringer: 86 (top). Allan Mandell: 73 (bottom). David McDonald: 37 (top). Jack McDowell: 99 (1–5). Owen McGoldrick: 85. Richard Nicol: 29, 31 (bottom), 43, 50. Gary W. Parker: 63, 64 (bottom). Norman A. Plate: 88 (all), 101 (top left and top right). Richard Ross: 34 (bottom right). Phil Schofield: 48 (top right). Tim Street-Porter: 34 (top). Dominique Vorillon: 56. Darrow M. Watt: 96–97 (bottom). Alan Weintraub/Arcaid: 78 (bottom). Tom Wyatt: 79, 108–109.

index

Page numbers in **boldface** refer to photographs